THE WELSH
GRAND NATIONAL

from *Deerstalker* to *Supreme Glory*

SECOND DAY

OFFICIAL PROGRAMME.

✻

PRICE

6D.

S. H. Wilton Pye

CARDIFF RACES

(UNDER NATIONAL HUNT RULES)

MONDAY AND TUESDAY,
APRIL 10TH AND 11TH, 1939

Patrons.

THE MARQUESS OF BUTE.
THE EARL OF PLYMOUTH.
THE VISCOUNT TREDEGAR.
LORD GLANELY.
THE MACKINTOSH OF MACKINTOSH.

Stewards.

LORD GLANELY.
C. C. WILLIAMS, Esq.,
ROBERT H. WILLIAMS, Esq.
THE VISCOUNT PORTMAN, M.F.H.

Officials.

Handicapper : Mr. R. TURNER. *Starter :* Mr. F. WILLIAMS.

Judge : Mr. JOHN COVENTRY.

Auctioneer : Mr. A. WILKINSON.

Clerk of the Scales : Mr. FRANK WOOD.

Club Secretary : Major S. B. WILDMAN, O.B.E., 5, High Street, Cardiff.

Medical Officers :

Dr. FREDERICK WILLIAM CAMPBELL, Physician and Surgeon, West Orchard, Llandaff.

Dr. G. E. LINDSAY, " Westcross," Penarth.

Veterinary Surgeons :

Mr. JOHN LORD PERRY, M.R.C.V.S., 58, Newport Road, Cardiff.

Mr. JAMES HAMILTON STEWART, M.R.C.V.S., 14, Neville Street, Cardiff.

Clerk of the Course and Stakeholder : Mr. T. H. WILTON PYE, Broad Street Chambers, 32, Broad Street, Worcester.

Prices (including Tax).

Course, 2/- ; Public Stand, 5/- ; Tattersalls : Gentlemen 12/6
Ladies 6/-.

Motors, 2/6 each, NOT including Occupants.

Western Mail & Echo Ltd., Cardiff.—2664F.

Official programme for Cardiff (Ely) Races 1939.

THE WELSH
GRAND NATIONAL

from *Deerstalker* to *Supreme Glory*

BRIAN LEE

TEMPUS

FOR PHILIP DONOVAN

First published 2002

PUBLISHED IN THE UNITED KINGDOM BY:
Tempus Publishing Ltd
The Mill, Brimscombe Port
Stroud, Gloucestershire GL5 2QG

PUBLISHED IN THE UNITED STATES OF AMERICA BY:
Tempus Publishing Inc.
2 Cumberland Street
Charleston, SC 29401

British Library Cataloguing in Publication Data.
A catalogue record for this book is available from the British Library.

ISBN 0 7524 2728 8

Typesetting and origination by Tempus Publishing.
Printed in Great Britain by Midway Colour Print, Wiltshire

CONTENTS

ACKNOWLEDGEMENTS

So many people have helped me with this book that lack of space prevents me from mentioning them all as I would have wished.

But I would like to express my special thanks to the following: Peter Scudamore MBE for writing the foreword; Paul Davies, of the *Complete Record*, for writing the introduction and compiling the race record; all those at Chepstow Racecourse for their help and encouragement; and Richard Lowther for providing me with past results of the Welsh Grand National.

Others I need to thank are Pat Lucas for allowing me to quote from her excellent book *Fifty Years Of Racing At Chepstow Racecourse*, the editors of the *Racing Post*, *The Sporting Life*, *The Western Mail*, *Horse and Hound*, *South Wales Echo* and *South Wales Argus* for publishing my requests for information and photographs and, of course, to all those readers who responded to them.

I would also like to thank the staff of the Local Studies Department, Cardiff Central Library, Rodger Farrant, Charles Hammond, Alan Wright, Geoffrey Hammonds, David Owen, Ernest Excell, Charles Fawcus, Gerry Cranham, Carl Burrows, Bill Smith and John Beasley; James Howarth, of Tempus Publishing, for helping me to realise my dream of putting on record the continuing story of the Welsh Grand National; and my grandson James Lee Harvey for helping me to get it all on to my computer.

Finally, I ask forgiveness from any contributors who may feel they have been omitted from these acknowledgements and, as it has not always been possible to trace copyright on some of the photographs, I apologize for any inadvertent infringement.

Brian Lee

FOREWORD

The Welsh Grand National – From Deerstalker to Supreme Glory is an engrossing study that not only documents the history of the great race, but also charts the development of National Hunt racing.

The various former venues of the race, Cardiff and Newport, are beautifully described in the book. The setting of today's Welsh National on the edge of the Wye Valley would rival that of any racecourse in the world.

The Welsh Grand National epitomises the spirit of National Hunt racing and many of the great steeplechasers have run in the race.

The book not only recalls the legendary trainers and jockeys that have won the race, but also the lesser known without whom National Hunt racing would not exist.

Peter Scudamore MBE

Peter Scudamore and Carvill's Hill, winner of the 1991 Welsh Grand National.

INTRODUCTION

One hundred and six years separate the victory of Deerstalker in the inaugural Welsh Grand National, and the success, last December, of Supreme Glory in the most recent renewal. During its long lifetime, the race has endured two World Wars, bankruptcy, the closure of not one but two courses, and some of the worst winter weather imaginable. But the event has survived and is now cherished as one of the highlights of the winter season.

The Welsh Grand National was, initially, a success, but within a few short years it became a luxury the cash-strapped Cardiff course could no longer afford. With the track under new management, the race returned in 1905, but for several years it languished as a lowly optional selling chase.

Between the wars, the race grew in stature, as steeplechasing benefited from the presence of such equine stars as Easter Hero, Reynoldstown and, of course, the immortal Golden Miller.

The gates to Cardiff racecourse remained locked after the war, while impoverished Newport, which staged one renewal, closed its doors for the final time in 1949. Happily the race moved to Chepstow that year, and over the last fifty-odd years it has gone from strength to strength.

It was John Hughes, Chepstow's innovative Clerk of the Course, who recognised that the Welsh Grand National had the potential to become a major player in the jumping season. So, in 1969, the race was moved from its traditional safe Easter Tuesday date to a far more vulnerable February slot.

The reward for this bold move came in 1976 when Rag Trade became the first horse to complete the Welsh and Aintree National double in the same season. The race was moved to its present position in the calendar in 1979, since when Corbiere and Earth Summit have emulated Rag Trade, while Burrough Hill Lad and Master Oats have completed the Welsh National/Cheltenham Gold Cup double.

Since 1979, the race has been run as the Welsh National. This is not a pedantic observation. Rather, the dropping of the word 'Grand' was a sign of the race's newfound confidence as a steeplechasing classic in its own right, not a parochial imitation of *the* Grand National.

It is fitting, therefore, that the story of Wales's greatest race is told by the country's foremost racing historian, Brian Lee. He has, I'm sure you'll agree, brought colour and life to this project. He has unearthed many wonderful tales from the past and has produced a work that will be referred to over and over again.

Paul Davies, *The Complete Record*

1895

As long ago as 1769, flat racing was taking place at Stalling Down in the Vale of Glamorgan. The Cardiff borough records contain references to race meetings at Heath Park, Cardiff, in the early 1800s, and by 1844 Welsh racegoers were well provided for with fixtures at Abergavenny, Monmouth, Wrexham and elsewhere.

Around this time, steeplechasing was coming into vogue all over the country and in Wales other meetings were to spring up at Cardiff, Tenby, Carmarthen and Pembroke. Of these fixtures the one at Cardiff's Ely Racecourse was to become the most important, attracting larger attendances and better class horses. This was chiefly due to the staging of the Cardiff Open Hunters' Steeplechase in 1877 which carried a prize of 100 sovereigns. This race, which was originally restricted to maiden hunters, became the Grand National Hunt Steeplechase in 1889 and the prize money was 440 sovereigns. It is from this race that the Welsh Grand National – now known as the Coral Eurobet Welsh National – evolved.

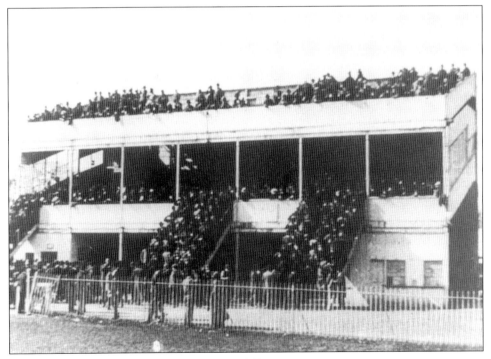

The old grandstand, Ely Racecourse, Cardiff.

Tom Cannon, who as a jockey had won the 1882 Derby on Shotover, and who had trained the 1888 Grand National winner Playfair, had the honour of owning the first Welsh Grand National winner Deerstalker. The distance of the race, which took place on Easter Monday, was around two-and-a-half miles and only seven of the twenty-one entries for the race faced the starter. For most of the way it was a two-horse race between seven-year-old Deerstalker and Dr Moyan's five-year-old Measure For Measure, ridden by the amateur Mr J. Lewis.

Red Saint was pulled up after breaking down and Barmecide fell at the second last fence past the stands and broke its neck. The hapless Barmecide over-jumped himself and turned a complete somersault causing his rider, W. Canavan, who incidentally had finished tenth in the Aintree National on Fin-Ma-Coul II, to have several teeth knocked out as well as a nasty wound to his forehead.

Deerstalker, enterprisingly ridden by George Mawson, who had been successful on Playfair at Aintree, jumped the last fence alongside Measure For Measure and drew away on the run-in to win by four lengths. Of the seven starters, these were the only finishers. Deerstalker was later sold to Mr Herbert Sarsfield Watson, a well known Cardiff businessman and sportsman who on a couple of occasions had won the Glamorgan Hunt Cup, the principal race at Cowbridge Steeplechases.

Tom Cannon, who has been described as, 'A slight and rather delicate-looking man with handsome features and bright intelligent eyes', had ridden 1,544 winners in his younger days. He had three sons and two of them, Mornington and Kempton, were first-class riders. The third, Thomas Leonard Gilbert, had taken over the training of his father's horses three years earlier in 1892.

Sadly, George Mawson, a former Flat race jockey of note, who switched codes when he became too heavy for the flat, had to hang up his riding boots after a very bad fall at Lingfield the following year. He never really recovered from his injuries and died in 1897 at the early age of thirty-two.

Monday 15 April 1895	£425		Two miles and four furlongs
1 Deerstalker (T. Cannon, Junior)		7-11-7	George Mawson
2 Measure For Measure (Dr R.M. Moyran)		5-11-2	Mr J. Lewis
Only two finished			

Winning owner Mr Tom Cannon

7 ran.   Distances: 4l.   SP evens fav., 5/1.

Deerstalker, bay gelding by Trappist-Antelope

More than 40,000 racegoers flocked to Ely Racecourse to see the 1892 Grand National winner Father O'Flynn take on the 1893 winner the legendary Cloister. The latter had won at Aintree with a record weight of 12st 7lb, in a record time and by a record distance of 40 lengths. Making practically all the running, Cloister won in a common canter by two lengths from Greenhill. Father O'Flynn, who had beaten Cloister by 20 lengths in the 1892 Grand National, was pulled up by Harry Escott, who later trained the 1909 Grand National winner Lutteur III, at the last fence when well out of contention.

Great Western railway poster for Cardiff Races, 1890.

Cloister's jockey Welshman Gwyn Saunders-Davies received a tremendous ovation and was lifted shoulder-high by some of his many Welsh supporters. Between 1882 and 1903 Saunders-Davies won 332 races and was placed in another 364 out of a total of 1,068 mounts. A popular performer of his was the mare Fairy Queen on whom he once won three races in two days, with the last two races within an hour of each other. Fairy Queen won many times at Ely Racecourse and her fine performance of winning six races within thirteen days must surely be a record of sorts. By Happy Land-Ethelreda, Fairy Queen won no fewer than forty-two races and apart from the occasion Saunders-Davies missed the train, he was aboard her in all her other victories.

Cloister's owner Charles Duff, a Caernarvonshire quarry owner, who in anticipation of a baronetcy changed his name to Charles Assheton-Smith in 1905, saw his colours carried to victory in two more Grand Nationals with Jerry M. (1912) and Covertcoat (1913). The *Western Mail* reported that, 'Mr Duff's Cloister looked in the pink of condition and from a broken down horse some eighteen months ago Mr Thompson, in whose care he has been until recently, had rejuvenated him, and turned out the old Grand National winner in tip top form.'

The Mr Thompson the paper referred to was Mr Charles Thompson who trained the old horse at Whaddon Chase after it had gone wrong and had collapsed in its preparation for the 1894 Grand National. Mr Thompson's skill and patience with the patched-up Cloister was a remarkable feat. No mean rider himself, Charles Thompson, or 'Bonnety Bob' as he was nicknamed owing to his family's connection with a millinery company, rode 45 winners in 1890 to win the amateur riders' championship.

Monday 6 April	£425		Two miles and four furlongs
1 Cloister (Charles Thompson)	12-11-10	Gwyn Saunders-Davies	
2 Greenhill (Wheeler)	5-10-10	E. Matthews	
3 Santa Rosa (Bustell)	a-10-10	C. James	

Winning owner Mr C.G. Duff

12 ran.   Distances: 2l, 10l.   SP 2/1 fav., 4/1, 5/1.

Cloister, bay gelding by Ascetic-Grace II

1897

A delightfully fine day is said to have brought the largest crowd to Ely Racecourse in years. However, of the original thirty-two entries just half-a-dozen of them faced the starter and these included Filbert who three weeks earlier had finished runner-up to the great Manifesto in the Aintree National.

Alterations and enlargement of the paddock, weighing room and jockeys' changing room provided a decided boom as the previous year the enclosures and stands had been packed to the point of making it uncomfortable for the thousands of racegoers pouring on to the course at Easter time.

The two fancied horses – Miss Battle and IOU – both disappointed. Miss Battle was a beaten horse half-a-mile from home and walked past the winning post in fourth and last place. IOU's jockey, Mr Lord, is reported to have taken the second obstacle 'like a bull at a gate' and crashed to earth. Mr G.R. Powell, riding his own horse Filbert, led into the straight, but a desperate challenge by Henry Brown on Mr E. Deacon's six-year-old Legal Tender saw him first past the post by a length.

Captain Morgan Lindsay's Dean Swift, ridden by Captain Lindsay's brother Walter, was a bad third. Filbert could be considered unlucky not to have won, for not only was he full of running at the finish, but his owner-rider had put up seven pounds overweight!

Monday 19 April	£425		Two miles and four furlongs
1 Legal Tender (privately)	6-11-10		Henry Brown
2 Filbert (Wilson)	7-10-10		Mr G.R. Powell
3 Dean Swift (privately)	9-11-10		Mr W. Lindsay

Winning owner Mr E. Deacon

6 ran.   Distances: 1l.   bad.   SP 6/1, 4/1, 10/1.   fav., 5-4.   IOU fell.

Legal Tender, bay gelding by Minting-Aureoline

1898

In contrast to the previous year, the weather for the 1898 Welsh Grand National was inclement to say the least. Nat Gould, who had won the Oakgrove Steeplechase over the old St Arvans Chepstow Racecourse a few days earlier, had his admirers but fell at the last open ditch. Two other casualties at this fence were the Irish challenger, Katabasis, who was travelling really well at the time, and the previous year's runner-up Filbert, who had been fourth in the 1898 Grand National a few weeks earlier. With these three fancied runners out of the way, a two-horse race developed between Mr F.W. Holden's aged Hedgehog and Frank Bibby's four-year-old Pyracantha. It was Hedgehog's challenge which prevailed by two lengths. Mr Straker's Stop, partnered by Arthur Gordon, was aptly named for after making the pace on the first circuit he quickly faded to finish a bad third.

Hedgehog, a 5/1 chance, was ridden by D. Davies who had also won the previous race – St Nicholas Hurdle – on Silent Watch by a head, beating the famed amateur rider Gwyn Saunders-Davies in a tight finish. D. Davies is recalled in Reggie Herbert's *When Diamonds Were Trumps*: 'Old Davies used, in his younger days, to ride most of Powell's horses. He was a rare hand over the Welsh courses, always carrying a ball of twine in his breeches pocket, fastened to his horse's bit, so that in case of a fall at one of the banks, and the horse getting loose, the line would pay out 'til Davies picked himself up, caught

The water jump at Ely Racecourse.

This is how the Cardiff Times artist depicted the bookmakers and punters in 1898.

hold of it, began hauling in the slack, and so brought his mount to hand, a fall over the sort of country they had to negotiate by no means extinguishing a winning chance.'

Hedgehog ran in the Glamorgan Steeplechase at the Cardiff November meeting and finished second to Fairy Queen with the first Welsh Grand National winner Deerstalker back in third place. This was no disgrace as Fairy Queen was chalking-up her thirty-seventh success. Fairy Queen, who had finished seventh in the 1897 Aintree National and who was to finish tenth in the 1899 race, never ran in the Welsh equivalent which seems a great pity as she certainly was capable of winning it.

Monday 11 April	£425	Two miles and four furlongs
1 Hedgehog (T. Spire)	a-11-4	D. Davies
2 Pyracantha (privately)	4-10-0	E. Morgan
3 Stop (J.G. Elsey)	a-12-2	Mr A. Gordon

Winning owner Mr F.W. Holden

10 ran.   Distances: 2l.   bad.   SP 5/1, 12/1, 2/1 fav.

Hedgehog, bay gelding, pedigree unknown

1899

The Western Mail reported that, 'The field for the Welsh Grand National was insignificant in point of numbers, although it was in no means lacking in class.'

Well, the winner Nat Gould, owned by Cardiff sportsman George Jukes, was a speedy sort having won the Ladies' Flat race over two miles at Cardiff the previous year. In the 1899 Welsh Grand National it was two fences from home that he joined Lambay in the lead and went on to win cleverly by two lengths from Slingsby.

Nat Gould's rider, Mr A.W. Wood, had a big following at Cardiff, Monmouth and Abergavenny, where his mounts usually started favourite – and won! Tall and lean in the saddle, he resembled the great Fred Archer. It was said that he only had one superior or equal in the Principality and that was Jack Goodwin. Joe Widger, who had finished down the field on Rays, had four years earlier won the Aintree National on Wild Man From Borneo and Finch Mason, who was also unplaced on Ben Armine, was champion jockey six times between 1901 and 1907. He went on to win the Aintree National on Welsh-trained Kirkland in 1905 and had he not broken a leg shortly before the 1911 race, he would have ridden the winner Glenside.

Captain W. Murray-Threipland, who finished third on Lambay, won the Household Brigade Cup, which was open to officers only, four times between 1893 and 1899 when he gave up race riding.

Monday 3 April	£425	Three miles
1 Nat Gould (Privately)	5-10-12	Mr A.W. Wood
2 Slingsby (Tudor)	7-10-12	Mr G.S. Davies
3 Lambay (Lawlor)	6-12-10	Mr W. Murray-Threipland

Winning owner Mr George Jukes

7 ran.   Distances: 2l, 2l.   SP 5/2, 5/1, 2/1 fav.

Nat Gould, bay gelding by Atholtas-British Queen

1900

Only six of the thirty-nine horses entered faced the starter for the 1900 Welsh Grand National. The Irish challenger, Captain Eustace Loder's Mena, was made joint-favourite with Mr R. Bourke's Bloomer but the latter, despite carrying top weight of 12st 10lb, shot to the front six furlongs from home to win easily by eight lengths from Mena to whom he was conceding more than two stone. The aged Granuale finished fourth, Heathvoe fell and Castleracket was pulled up.

Bloomer, an eight-year-old chestnut gelding, was as tough as old boots and won 22 races including the Grand Sefton and Champion Chase. Bloomer's rider, A. Banner, had ridden Mr Bourke's Whiteboy II into sixth place in the previous year's Aintree National.

Monday 16 April	£425	Three miles
1 Bloomer (Green)	8-12-10	A. Banner
2 Mena (In Ireland)	a-9-8	A. Anthony
3 Spinning Boy (Lukie)	a-10-9	Collard

Winning owner Mr R. Bourkes

6 ran.   Distances: 8l, 8l.   SP 6/4 jt. fav., 6/4 jt. fav., 5/1.

Bloomer, chestnut gelding by Blue Grass-Skeffington

Ivor Anthony, who trained Welsh Grand National winners Boomlet and Pebble Ridge, is seen here with that legendary pair, Brown Jack and Steve Donaghue.

1901

'The race for the Welsh Grand National was one of the least interesting of the day', wrote *The Western Mail*'s racing correspondent. There were only four runners out of an entry of twenty-eight and Gangbridge, partnered by his owner, Herbert S. Sidney, won in a common canter by fifteen lengths from Frank Bibby's Kirkland, ridden by E. Morgan. Colonel Freddie Morgan's Pathetic finished a bad third while the only other runner, Spread Eagle, fell a mile from the finish. Mr Sidney, the Cheltenham amateur rider, who had been the leading jockey the previous season with a total of 53 winners, later made it a treble by winning the Penllyn Selling Hurdle on his Hainesby Rouge and the Green Meadow Steeplechase on Mr Green's Tom Tit. Sadly, Mr Sidney was killed in a race riding accident at Dunstall Park the following year.

Five-year-old Kirkland, trained by Freddie Lort Phillips at Lawrenny Park in Pembrokeshire, went on to win 10 races, including the Grand Sefton, but his finest moment came in 1905 when he won the Aintree National and to this day remains the only horse actually trained in Wales to have won the world's greatest steeplechase. One person who remembered Colonel Lort Phillips was Miss F.M. Prior, author of several books on the breeding of thoroughbreds. She reminisced, 'I spent many happy days at Lawrenny Castle as the guest of Colonel and Mrs Lort Phillips. I believe the castle was pulled down some years later and transferred to Pembroke to assist with its materials in making the dock there, but the whole structure fell into the sea.' She added, 'I do recall that the Colonel put my name forward to act as a judge at the Tenby Show and that one of the Anthony brothers who was in charge of the proceedings turned the suggestion down on the grounds that I was a woman!'

Monday 8 April	£410		Three miles
1 Gangbridge (J. Goode)	8-11-9	Mr H.S. Sidney	
2 Kirkland (Colonel F. Lort-Phillips)	5-10-12	E. Morgan	
3 Pathetic (Privately)	6-10-9	Mr S.P. Christy	

Winning owner Mr H.S. Sidney

4 ran.   Distances: 15l.   bad.   SP 1/3 fav., 4/1, 10/1.

Gangbridge, chestnut gelding by Cylinder-Squabble.

1905

The fact that Mr Lewis Gottwaltz resigned his secretaryship of Ely Racecourse – a post he had held for seventeen years – in 1902 was probably the main reason why there were no Welsh Grand Nationals between 1902 and 1904. He claimed that the people of South Wales had not the love of horse racing which was found in other parts of the country and it is true that attendance figures were on the decline.

However, now under the management of Messrs Pratt, the racecourse was in a more prosperous condition and, for the first time in its existence, the directors were able to declare a dividend of 5 per cent in 1904. So after an absence of three years the race was revived and took place on the Easter Tuesday instead of the usual Easter Monday fixture.

The race was also reduced to an optional selling race in which all horses claimed to be sold at £50 – and the winner Glenrocky was one of them – were given 10st 10lb to carry whilst those horses not for sale were handicapped separately. Heavy rain fell during the day which made the going very heavy and minimised the attendance.

This is how the *South Wales Echo* described the race, 'Most Excellent from Glenrocky, Slipthrift and Crautacaun, with Sanguinetti last, showed the way for nearly two miles, when the leader dropped to the rear and was soon pulled up. Six furlongs from home Crautacaun took a slight lead of Glenrocky, and soon after Slipthrift fell, leaving Glenrocky to win by two lengths from Creolin with Sanguinetti a bad third. Crautacaun was remounted to finish fourth.'

Sanguinetti's rider, Captain Rasbotham, a fortnight earlier had won the Scottish Grand National at Eglinton on Mr Bower Ismay's Theodocian and Glenrocky, who had run in the same race, finished among the also rans. Glenrocky, ridden by F. Barter, was rather a lucky winner as Crautacaun was well in front when he fell at the penultimate fence. The winner, who was trained by a Mr Baker at Weyhill, was bought in for 220 guineas.

Owen Anthony, who trained the immortal Golden Miller, with his private secretary Francis Carter.

Tuesday 25 April	**£410**	**Three miles**

1	Glenrocky (W.R. Baker)	a-10-10	Frank Barter
2	Creolin (Colonel Morgan Lindsay)	8-11-3	Mr O. Anthony
3	Sanguinetti (Privately)	6-11-3	Captain Rasbotham

Winning owner Mr David Faber

4 ran.   Distances: 2l.   SP 6/4 fav., 8/1, 3/1.   Going very heavy.

Glenrocky, bay gelding by Glenvannon-Frances

1906

Only four horses sported silk for the 1906 Welsh Grand National. Ivor Anthony, aged twenty-three, having won the earlier novice steeplechase on Dinna Ben and the selling hurdle on Lady Patty, had high hopes of a hat-trick when he rode down to the start on the favourite Sunstroke II. When the second-favourite, Mr Francis Porter Gilbert's Shoeblack, which had recent winning form at Leicester, Birmingham and Plumpton, refused to race at the start he must have thought it was his lucky day. However, Shoeblack, an eight-year-old black gelding, after giving the remaining three runners 'a field's length start', chased after them with such gusto that he had caught them up by the second circuit.

Throughout the race, Sunstroke II never really looked like winning and the top-weighted Shoeblack, under Mr Arthur W. Wood, who had been successful on Nat Gould in 1899, eventually won by three lengths from the rank outsider Chilumchee, ridden by Cardiff jockey Freddie Parker, who just pipped Sunstroke II by a head for second place.

The previous year's winner, Glenrocky, again ridden by Frank Barter, failed to complete the course. Shoeblack, a former hunter who had won his previous two races, was trained by his owner at East Isley in Berkshire. Freddie Parker's claim to fame was that he won the Glamorgan Hunt Cup at nearby Cowbridge Steeplechases three times – in 1904 on Amulet, in 1905 on Domb Nut and in 1907 on Bella III.

Tuesday 17 April		£410		Three miles
1	Shoeblack (Mr Francis Porter Gilbert)		8-11-3	Mr Arthur Wood
2	Chilumchee (Hon. A. Hastings)		7-10-10	F. Parker
3	Sunstroke II (R Smith)		a-10-10	I. Anthony

Winning owner Mr Francis Porter Gilbert

4 ran.   Distances: 3l.   bad.   SP 2/1, 10/1, 11/10 fav.

Shoeblack, black horse by Common-Bluemark

1908

There was no Welsh Grand National in 1907. This was the year that Ivor Anthony won the Scottish Grand National on the Tenby-trained Atrato, who got home by a head from Rory O. Moore. As for the Welsh equivalent, according to *The Western Mail* the race 'was the tit-bit of the meeting and doubtless accounted for the large and aristocratic attendance in the club enclosure, which was certainly the best seen in connection with the gathering'.

In contrast the *South Wales Daily News* reported that, 'The Welsh Grand National was not a great race.' The winner, Captain R.H. Fowler's Razorbill, who at five was the youngest horse in the race, is said to have owed his success to a blunder by Frank Bibby's Rex at the water jump.

Prince Hatzfeldt's The Leek flattered only to deceive at two miles, and Lord Ninian Crichton Stuart's Clean Linen, if you will excuse the pun, was out with the washing finishing in tenth and last place, much to the disappointment of his owner, the parliamentary candidate for Cardiff, who was sadly later to be killed in action in the First World War.

Razorbill, trained by D. Maher at Winchester, and ridden by Bartholomew Flannery, cleared the last fence slightly ahead of Rex, ridden by Walter Bulteel and Gabriel II, ridden by Mr Harry Brown and they finished in that order. Walter Bulteel, who worked at the Stock Exchange, was one of the best amateur riders of his day and had more than 100 winners to his credit and he had ridden the first of them at Torquay in 1896.

Little is known of the winning rider Bartholomew Flannery, but Harry Atherton Brown, who finished third on Gabriel II, was the younger brother of Frank Atherton Brown and both were very good cross country jockeys. The favourite, The Leek, finished fourth.

Harry, aged nineteen, who had ridden his first winner the previous season, was to become the leading amateur rider four times between 1918-21, and in 1919 he was also champion jockey when riding a remarkable 48 winners.

One of the sport's great characters, he was unlucky not to have won the Aintree National. When Troytown won the 1920 race he finished third on The Bore and then in 1921 the partnership came second to Shaun Spadah. The Bore had fallen two fences from home when disputing the lead, and despite a broken collar bone Brown had remounted to claim the runner up spot and some hefty wagers he had made to finish in the frame. On a horse called Dudley, which he also trained, he won fourteen consecutive races. The character, Charlie Peppercorn, in Sassoon's *Memoirs of a Foxhunter Man* is said to have been based on him.

Horses being unboxed at Ely station.

Tuesday 21 April	**£337**	**Three miles**
1 Razorbill (D. Maher)	5-10-10	Bernard Flannery
2 Rex (Donnelly)	6-10-3	Mr W. Bulteel
3 Gabriel II (Hallick)	a-10-10	Mr H.A. Brown

Winning owner Captain R.H. Fowler

11 ran.   Distances: 3l, ½l.   SP 7/1, 4/1, 5/1   Fav., The Leek 3/1.

Razorbill, chestnut gelding by Red Prince II-Greenshank

1909

Mr W.F. Stratton's six-year-old Roman Candle, a 10/1 chance, under Elisha Ward, came with a rare late rattle to win the 1909 Welsh Grand National by a head from the favourite Mr W.B. Partridge's Timothy Titus. Although carrying a stone less than the winner, this was still a good performance as Timothy Titus was no mean performer having won the 1904 National Hunt Chase when ridden by Ivor Anthony.

The narrow defeat of the runner-up came as a great disappointment to his sixty-nine-year-old owner, businessman William Bailey Partridge, who had his own private pack of hounds and who resided at Bacton in Herefordshire. While living at Llanfoist near Abergavenny, he had bred Madame Nerida II who had won the Epsom Great Metropolitan and many other races. Timothy Titus, a handsome steeplechaser, was bred by John Anthony, father of the famed Anthony brothers. Frank Bibby's Breemount, who was a distant third, was ridden by Captain Robert Henry Collis D.S.O. who had been an officer in the 6th Dragoon Guards during the Boer War. In 1907 he had ridden Napper Tandy to eighth place in the Aintree National and he had many successes at the Sandown Park Military meeting. Perhaps his biggest success was when he won the National Hunt Steeplechase at Warwick, on Comfit, for Mr Bibby, in 1905.

Tuesday 13 April	£377	Three miles

1	Roman Candle (Mr W.F. Stratton)	7-10-10	Elisha Ward
2	Timothy Titus (Morgan)	11-11-10	J. Walsh, junior
3	Breemount (Donnelly)	7-10-10	Captain R.H. Collis

Winning owner Mr W.F. Stratton

7 ran.   Distances: head.   bad.   SP 10/1, 2/1 fav., 4/1.

Roman Candle, chestnut gelding by Robertson-Fireworks

1910

Some more alterations were made to Ely Racecourse in time for the 1910 renewal. The stands in the public enclosure had been entirely rebuilt and remodelled to hold double the number of visitors and for the first time the entire racecourse was railed all the way round. Entrance to the public stands was three shillings while five shillings would have got you into Tattersalls. Entrance to the course, however, was still a shilling.

There were only six starters, and two of them, Frank Bibby's Caubeen and Mr A. Law's Fetler's Pride, had earlier ran in the Aintree National. The former had finished in fifth and last place and the latter had been knocked over at the fence before Becher's Brook. The weather was said to be 'glorious' and the crowd large. Caubeen's rider Finch Mason, who had been brought down from Manchester foregoing an important engagement there, took up the running a mile from home to win comfortably by eight lengths from Fetler's Pride, partnered by P. Gilligan, with Mr E. Shrimpton's Whitecliffe, ridden by Paddy Cowley, a bad third.

The second favourite Onward, ridden by J. Walsh junior, had looked to have some sort of chance before falling on the second circuit. Liverpool-born Mason was something of a rough diamond. He had been champion jockey on the flat in Ireland before coming to Britain to ride over the sticks. He had headed the list of leading riders six times between 1901 and 1907.

Usually seen wearing a cloth cap and his favourite old dark blue overcoat the clichés, 'cool as a cucumber' and 'brave as a lion' fitted him admirably. Of the old school of riders, he rode rather long. In contrast, Paddy Cowley rode a lot shorter than any of the jockeys of his era and was probably years ahead of his time.

This unassuming Irishman beat Mason for the jockeys' championship in 1908, but his career came to an abrupt and tragic end when he was killed after he smashed his skull in a race riding accident at Hooton Park shortly afterwards.

Tuesday 29 March		£337	Three miles
1	Caubeen (Donnelly)	9-10-12	Finch Mason
2	Fetlar's Pride (E.D. Gwilt)	9-12-0	P. Gilligan
3	Whitecliffe (Brogden)	a-11-10	P. Cowley

Winning owner Mr Frank Bibby

6 ran.   Distances: 8l.   bad.   SP 6/4 fav., 5/1, 6/1.

Caubeen, brown horse by Chad-Revenue Cutter

1911

This year's Aintree National winner, the one-eyed Glenside, figured among the entries for the 1911 Welsh equivalent but was wisely taken out of the race at the final declaration stage. In winning at Liverpool he had been the only horse to complete the course without falling and had finished in a very distressed condition. It was only Jack Anthony's sympathetic handling and his supreme horsemanship that got Glenside home twenty lengths clear of the remounted Rathnally.

Jack's brother, Ivor Anthony, was reported to have ridden one of the best races of his life in winning this year's race. Riding the top-weighted Razorbill, who had been successful three years earlier, he came from a long way behind to snatch victory at the winning post from Mr G.L. Pirie's Flaxen, a faller at Liverpool, to whom he conceded 9lb.

Ivor Anthony (1883-1959) won the 1911 Welsh Grand National on Razorbill.

Jack Anthony, on Frank Bibby's Aerostat, finished a further fifteen lengths away in third place. Glencat and Inchquin both fell first time round and Coiffure refused a mile from home. Now running in the colours of Mr R. Ashton, Razorbill had the distinction of become the first dual winner of the Welsh Grand National. On this occasion he was trained by Percy Whitaker at Royston. Captain Whitaker, who had headed the list of winning amateur riders with 26 winners in 1908, could have been unlucky not to have won that year's Grand National as the horse he was riding, The Lawyer III, dropped dead after finishing third to Rubio and Mattie Macgregor. The same year he had won the National Hunt Chase on Rory O'Moore. He was also the trainer of Silvo, who in 1925 won the Grand Steeplechase de Paris with F.B. Rees in the saddle.

Tuesday 18 April	£337		Three miles
1 Razorbill (P.G. Whitaker)	8-12-9	Ivor Anthony	
2 Flaxen (G.L. Pirie)	9-12-0	Mr A. Smith	
3 Aerostat (Launchbury)	a-11-12	Mr J.R. Anthony	

Winning owner Mr R. Ashton
8 ran.   Distances: head, 15l.   SP 2/1 fav., 5/1, 3/1.
Razorbill, chestnut gelding by Red Prince II-Greenshank

1912

Frank Lyall, the eldest of five steeplechasing brothers, had some consolation for having finished second on Bloodstone in this year's Aintree National when he won the 1912 Welsh Grand National on Mr C. Bower-Ismay's Jacobus. A five-year-old, whose previous wins had been over hurdles, Jacobus outjumped his five rivals despite the fact that he was running in a steeplechase for the first time. Had there been a best turned-out award in those days, Jacobus, who went on to finish runner-up to Ally Sloper in the 1915 Aintree marathon, would almost certainly have won it. He was much admired in the parade ring and it came as no surprise when he stormed home an easy three-lengths winner ahead of Lord Suffolk's General Fox, ridden by Herbert William Tyrwhitt-Drake. The previous year, 1911, Mr Tyrwhitt-Drake had been the leading amateur rider with 50 wins from 188 mounts. Born at Thornton Hall near Buckingham in 1886, and a member of the famous Tyrwhitt-Drake family of Shardeloes, Amersham, he was sadly killed in action in the First World War.

Frank Lyall's brother, George Lyall, was third on Captain C. de Wiart's Quinton, who finished a further half-a-length away. George Lyall went on to win the 1931 Aintree National on Grakle. Jacobus was trained by that controversial racing character Tom Coulthwaite who amazingly had never sat on a horse in his life! Be that as it may, it didn't stop him training three Grand National winners in Eremon (1907), Jenkinstown (1910) and Grakle (1931). The

Tom Coulthwaite who trained the 1912 Welsh Grand National winner, Jacobus.

Tom Coulthwaite is seen left of picture walking behind his favourite horse Grakle ridden by Jack Fawcus.

following year, 1913, the stewards of the National Hunt Committee enquired into the running of Jacobus at Birmingham and Bloodstone at Hurst Park. Not satisfied with the explanation they were given as to his horses' inconsistent form, Coulthwaite was warned off. He was given his licence back in 1920 and trained many more winners and has even been honoured by having a race named after him which is run at Haydock.

Tuesday 9 April	£350		Three miles
1 Jacobus (T. Coulthwaite)	5-11-6	Frank Lyall	
2 General Fox (F. Hartigan)	8-12-5	Mr H.T. Drake	
3 Quinton (Capt. C. de Wiart)	a-11-10	G.W. Lyall	

Winning owner Mr C. Bower Ismay

6 ran.   Distances: 3l, ½l   SP 2/1 fav., 3/1, 4/1.

Jacobus, bay gelding by Wavelet's Pride-Kendaline

1914

There had been no Welsh Grand National in 1913 and of the twenty-one entries for the 1914 race, only four of them went to post. Freddie Parker's Dick Dunn, with Sam Walkington in the saddle, was made an odds-on favourite with Freddy Lort Phillips's Succubus, who a fortnight earlier had won the County Handicap Hurdle at Monmouth, the 7/1 rank outsider.

Despite the small field, the race was run at a cracking pace and at the last fence Dick Dunn landed ahead of Succubus. However, Succubus's jockey, Charlie Kelly, riding like the devil himself, put in such a strong challenge on the run-in that he forced the judge to declare a dead heat.

Sir George Bullough's Simon The Lepper, ridden by Ivor Anthony, finished some three lengths back in third place. Lort Phillips, one of the acting stewards at the meeting, was quite willing to share the prize money with Mr Parker but he would not agree to do so. So, as was the custom in those days, the pair re-ran the race after the last event had been decided.

Odds of 1/2 were laid on Dick Dunn, but after they had crawled for the first furlong or so, Succubus, at the turn past the stands, suddenly spurted ahead with a ten-lengths lead which he maintained to the winning post. Succubus apparently ended up running in point-to-points. His rider, Charlie Kelly, who had finished second on Red Lad in the 1906 Aintree National won by Ascetic's Silver, was, according to Frank Atherton Brown, one of the finest schooling jockeys of his day. No horse he ever sat on had a chance of refusing a fence and he was said to have taken great delight in riding the chanciest of jumpers.

Tuesday 14 April	£350		Three miles and 100 yards
1 Succubus (F. Lort Phillips)	6-11-3	Charlie Kelly
1 Dick Dunn (Kelly)	a-11-12	S.B. Walkington
3 Simon The Lepper (Hon. A. Hastings)	5-11-6	I. Anthony

Winning owners F. Lort Phillips and Mr F. Parker
4 ran.   Distances: dead-heat   SP 7/1, 8/13 fav., 9/2.
Succubus won the re-run by 10l.   SP 2/1.

1920

The first post-war Welsh Grand National carried a first prize of 460 sovereigns – just 35 sovereigns more than Deerstalker's connections had received for winning the very first Welsh Grand National back in 1895! There were nine runners and Herbert Smyth, riding Mark Back, took up the running a mile from home to win by two lengths from the favourite, the locally-trained Mother's Gift who, the day before, had won the Glanely Novices Steeplechase over the course for owner Mr Watkins Williams.

This is how the *South Wales News* described the race, 'The titbit of the day was the Welsh Grand National. Nine ran. At the second fence Mother's Gift led from The Fly II, and The Trout with the remainder of the field close up. Twister blundered and unseated Kelly and interfered with Schoolmoney who was tailed off. At two miles Mark Back came to the front with The Fly II in close attendance on Mother's Gift who at the distance challenged, but Mark Back went on to win and finished first in a fine race by two lengths from Mother's Gift. The Fly II was third three lengths away and Sticktoit fourth. Schoolmoney broke down.' Mark Back was owned by Mr Ernest Mills, later to become Sir Ernest Mills the tobacco king. Captain Radclyffe's The Fly II, under Robert Gordon, was a further three lengths back in third place. Robert Gordon, who headed the list of winning riders in 1909, was known as 'The Blue Monkey' owing to his gremlin-like features and permanent seven o'clock shadow.

As for Herbert Smyth, Roger Mortimer in *The History of Steeplechasing* had this to say, 'Herbert Smyth was not only very able professionally, but had a considerable wit and many of his sayings, unfortunately unrepeatable here, have deservedly won a permanent place in the lore and legend of racing.'

Mother's Gift's jockey, Henry Bryan Bletsoe, had twelve years earlier won the Aintree National on 66/1 chance Rubio who at one time pulled the hotel bus at the Prospect Arms in Towcester.

Tuesday 6 April	£367		Three miles
1 Mark Back (G.S. de Winton)	9-11-9	Herbert Smyth	
2 Mother's Gift (H.B. Bletsoe)	a-10	H.B. Bletsoe	
3 The Fly III (R. Gordon)	13-12-4	R. Gordon	

Winning owner Mr E. Wills

9 ran.   Distances: 2l, 3l.   SP 3/1, 6/4 fav., 6/1.   Going good.

Mark Back, chestnut horse by Marcovil-Oliveback

1921

Prize money for the 1921 Welsh Grand National was more than double what it had been the previous year. An extra stand had been built with new luncheon- and tea-rooms and a dozen turnstiles were put up at the entrance to prevent congestion. The paddock was improved and a new draining system installed.

National Hunt racing was certainly popular in South Wales and at the Glamorgan Hunt Steeplechases at Cowbridge, held a few weeks earlier, more than 30,000 racegoers had been admitted. Roger Burford, later to be associated with the famed Brown Jack, won this year's race on Mr W.A. Bankier's Mythical who finished two-and-a-half lengths clear of Mrs Blain's Clonree whose rider, Tom Hulme, carried top weight of 12st 2lb. Major F.S. Murray's Gerald L, ridden by Ivor Anthony, was a further fifteen lengths away in third.

The aged Gerald L, who had won the National Hunt Chase at Cheltenham, proved what a good sort he was when finishing a close third in the first Cheltenham Gold Cup three years later, beaten a head and a neck by Red Splash and Conjuror II. Mythical was trained by Aubrey Hastings at Wroughton, who was the third son of the 13th Earl of Huntingdon. He trained and rode the 1906 Aintree National winner Ascetic's Silver and also trained three other Grand National winners in Ally Sloper (1915), Ballymacad (1917) and Master Robert (1924).

Mr Bankier, who was from Wantage, Berkshire, had a number of good horses with Hastings and these included Forewarned, who was usually ridden by Jack Anthony. His son, Captain A. Bankier, rode as an amateur and went as assistant trainer to Jack Anthony in 1928.

Roger Burford had finished second on The Turk II in the 1920 Aintree National behind Jack Anthony's mount Troytown. Burford's son, also named Roger, a jockey of renown, won the 1941 Cheltenham Gold Cup on Poet Prince.

Tuesday 29 March	£860		Three miles and four furlongs
1 Mythical (Hon. A. Hastings)	7-10-6		Roger Burford
2 Clonree (P. Whitaker)	7-12-2		T. Hulme
3 Gerald L (E.D. Gwilt)	7-11-5		I. Anthony

Winning owner Mr W.A. Bankier

10 ran.   Distances: 2½l, 14l.   SP 7/2 jt. fav., 9/2, 7/2 jt. fav.   Going good.

Mythical, brown gelding by Myram-Lady Superior

1922

There was record money for the year's race with 1,000 sovereigns going to the winner, 150 sovereigns to the second and fifty sovereigns to the third. Mythical, this time ridden by Jack Anthony, was made a 2/1 favourite to repeat last year's success. Unfortunately though, he was involved in a false start and, along with several other horses, he completed nearly a circuit of the course before the jockeys were aware that anything was wrong. Some of the riders had thought that the starter, Fred Williams, whose son Evan was to win the 1937 Aintree National on Royal Mail, had shouted 'Go' when he had in fact shouted 'Whoa'. One of the first horses to feel the effects of the false start when the race eventually got under way was the Irish challenger Mask On who faded on entering the straight. And when Mythical challenged Mr M.G. Dobbyn's Simonides, ridden by Thomas Willmot, close home he could make no impression.

When the winning post was reached Simonides, who used to be trained by Henry Bletsoe at East Isley, but who was now in the care of Alexander Cox, had two-and-a-half lengths to spare over Mr T. Galletly's Confessor, ridden by F. Croney, with the unfortunate Mythical a further head behind in third place. L.B. Rees, who had won this year's Aintree National on Music Hall, finished among the also-rans on Sir Harry Webb's Bubbly, who two days later won the Abertillery Handicap Steeplechase at Newport, Caerleon races.

Alexander Cox, the first son of a Liverpool jute merchant, inherited his brother Alfred's fortune when he died in 1919. Alfred, who was known on the turf as 'Mr Fairie', made a fortune in Australia when he discovered silver on a derelict sheep farm he had won in a poker game. On his return to England, ten years later, he bred Gay Crusader who won the Triple Crown in 1917. He turned down an offer of £100,000 for the horse shortly before he died.

Tuesday 18 April	£800		Three miles and four furlongs
1 Simonides (A.E. Cox)		8-10-5	Thomas Willmot
2 Confessor (A.H. Saxby)		8-10-12	F. Croney
3 Mythical (Hon. A. Hastings)		8-11-3	J. Anthony

Winning owner Mr M.G. Dobbyn

10 ran.   Distances: 2½l, head.   SP 10/1,10/1, 2/1 fav.

Simonides, bay gelding by Simon Square-Singlet

1923

For the first time in the history of the race a woman owner, Mrs A. Blaine, was successful. Clonree, ridden by J. Hogan, junior, scored by one-and-a-half lengths from Mr W. Edwards's Grey Dawn V with Mr G. Sanday's Jimmu a further two lengths back in third place.

The first three jumped the last almost together, but it was Clonree the 5/2 favourite who found the better speed on the run-in, to the delight of the large crowd. Three of the twelve starters – Punt Gun, Pencoed and Shaun Spadah – who figured among the also-rans were Aintree survivors. Shaun Spadah, this year's Becher Chase winner, had won the 1921 Aintree National under the incomparable Fred 'Dick' Rees. An objection to the second horse by the rider of the third on the grounds of foul riding was overruled.

Dr Mona C. Davies, Mr Elystan Bowen Davies and Mrs Catherine Bowen Davies enjoying a day at Cardiff races, c. 1930.

Of J. Hogan, junior, who had finished sixth at Aintree on Max, Welsh jockey David L. Jones, in Pat Lucas's *Fifty Years of Racing at Chepstow*, had this to say: 'He was a great character, a very colourful dresser – wore his clothes up to the minute just like a fashion plate. He always carried a rolled umbrella on his arm with a leather handle and a gold band round it. He wore his collar open, with a blue spotted cravat, and always looked immaculate. As a jockey he was quite brilliant. When he was in a London hospital, he requested a last trip to see the lights, and he got it. John, Michael Beary's brother, took him, and about two days after that he died.'

Clonree, a nine-year-old, was trained by a gentleman called Spittle at Letcombe Basset. David Purvis Dick, who rode Decco into fifth place, was the father of swashbuckling Dave Dick who was to win the 1956 Aintree National on ESB. Mr Dick senior had started out as a Flat race jockey, but increasing weight problems forced him to ride over-the-sticks. Following a bad fall he began training in 1929 at Epsom where he sent out many winners. Ely Racecourse in those days was described as the Ascot of Wales and this is what the woman

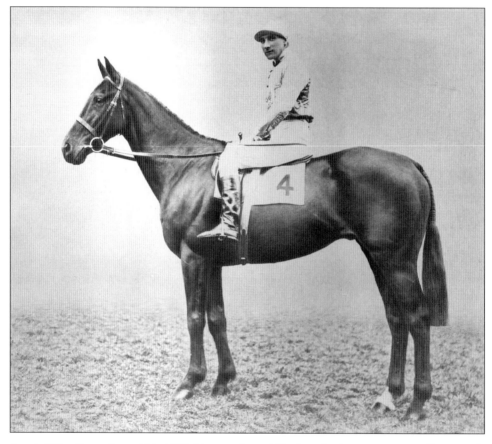

Lewis Bilby Rees aboard his 1922 Aintree Grand National winner Music Hall. He rode Shaun Spadah in the 1923 Welsh Grand National.

W. Parvin, who rode in the
Welsh Grand National a record
eleven times.

fashion correspondent of *The Western Mail* had to say of the fashions that were very much in evidence: 'The toilettes worn by the ladies were worthy of the glorious sunshine, and some wonderful creations were seen in the paddock and members' enclosure. The dresses provided a pageant of colour and form, and were expressive of fashion's latest dictates.'

Tuesday 3 April	£785	Three miles and four furlongs

1	Clonree (G. Spittle)	9-11-6	J. Hogan jnr
2	Grey Dawn V (Piggott)	10-11-1	C. Kelly
3	Jimmu (G.P. Sanday)	9-11-7	F. Mason

Winning owner Mrs A. Blain

12 ran.   Distances: 1½l, 2l.   SP 5/2 fav., 100/8, 10/1.   Going good.

Clonree, bay gelding by Atlas-Miss Eager

It was in 1924 that the National Hunt Committee, together with the Prestbury Park executive, instituted the Cheltenham Gold Cup which was won by Fred 'Dick' Rees on Red Splash. The value to the winner of the race was just £685 whereas prize money for this year's Welsh Grand National was £1,000.

Mr H. Liddell's Winnall, who a few weeks earlier had led the field a merry dance in the Aintree National until falling out in the country on the second circuit, was made a 2/1 favourite. However, he fell at the first fence after trying to refuse to jump the obstacle.

Mr H. Kennard's Dwarf of the Forest, ridden by former Flat race jockey R.G. Calder, was in a prominent position throughout the race and the Newmarket-trained 10/1 chance easily held off the challenge of Mr C. Clarke's Bodyguard, ridden by Roger Burford, by three lengths. A further two lengths back in third spot was Sir Harry Webb's Mr Madcap, partnered by D. Behan.

This win was the highlight of Calder's riding career although as an apprentice he had won the Newbury Spring Cup on Preferment. He rode chiefly for W. Saxby's Cheltenham yard and for Exining trainer Samuel Bennett. Sadly, he died of cancer just three years later at the early age of thirty-three. Bob Trudgill, who had won this year's Aintree National on Master Robert, finished among the also-rans on Mr W.A. Bankier's Ellendune. A west-countryman who would never refuse any ride offered to him, this gritty freelance jockey had many bad falls during his riding career. In fact the day before he rode Master Robert to victory he received a crashing fall which necessitated him having his leg stitched.

Ignoring the racecourse doctor's advice, he weighed out for the race and during the race the stitches burst open. But the brave Trudgill waited until he had dismounted in the winner's enclosure before collapsing. Billy Stott, who was to become champion jockey from 1927 to 1932, had a bad fall from Lord Coventry's Dart and was badly injured when several horses trod on him.

Dwarf of the Forest, a seven-year-old former hunter chaser, was trained by twenty-six-year-old Sam Bennett, an ex-amateur rider who had served with the Norfolk regiment in France during the Great War. After the hostilities he started training and saddled his first winner at Kempton in 1920. He used to train at Exining, but after the death of his brother, Captain G.H. 'Toppy' Bennett, he took over his Newmarket yard.

*Ivor Anthony rode the 1911
winner Razorbill.*

Tuesday 22 April	£785	Three miles and four furlongs

1	Dwarf of the Forest (S. Bennett)	7-10-5	R.C. Calder
2	Bodyguard (Hon. A. Hastings)	10-10-12	R. Burford
3	Mr Madcap (D. Harrison)	7-11-0	D. Behan

Winning owner Mr Kennard

11 ran.   Distances: 3l, 2l..   SP 10/1, 10/1, 10/1.   Fav. Winnal 2/1 refused.

Going good.

Dwarf of the Forest, by The Giant-Blackbird

1925

Mrs W.H. Dixon's Old Tay Bridge, who had finished second to Double Chance in this year's Aintree National, beaten just three lengths, was made a 3/1 favourite to win this year's race. But this very unlucky horse – he was also destined to be runner-up in the Aintree National and Cheltenham Gold Cup the following year – was soundly trounced in the heavy ground by Vaulx, a former hunter chaser. This good stayer, who had cost just £10 as a yearling, was ridden by Keith Piggott, the father of the legendary Lester Piggott.

Owned and trained by Keith's uncle, Charles Piggott, Vaulx jumped the last fence alongside Old Tay Bridge, ridden by Jack Anthony, but on the run-in drew away to win by ten lengths. A further five lengths away in third spot was Mr W. Parsonage's Master Billie partnered by G. Turner. Vaulx was named after the village of Vaulx-Vraucourt on the Somme where Charles Piggott had been stationed during the Great War. This eleven-year-old brown gelding had won the National Hunt Chase at Cheltenham in 1922 and 1924. As well as his success in the Welsh Grand National, twenty-one-year-old Keith Piggott went on to win the 1927 Grand Sefton on Trump Card and the 1939 Champion Hurdle on African Sister.

He rode 350 winners all told and has the distinction of riding the very last winner at Ely Racecourse in 1939 on Grasshopper. His biggest success as a trainer was when he won the 1963 Aintree National with 66/1 chance Ayala for hairdresser 'Teasy-Weasy' Raymond. Keith Piggott's father, Ernie Piggott, who died at the age of eighty-eight, was one of the best steeplechase jockeys of his day. He was champion jockey on three occasions and rode around 1,000 winners. He also won the Aintree National on Jerry M in 1912 and on Poethlyn in 1918.

Recalling the race, in Chris Pitt's *A Long Time Gone*, Keith Piggott had this to say, 'Vaulx was trained by my uncle Charlie at Cheltenham. He jocked Fred Rees off because he thought he'd carved him up in a race at the Cheltenham Festival Meeting. I was only twenty but he put me up, even though I'd just had a few rides over fences. I recall we met a funeral on the way to the course and we both thought 'that's done it'. I tracked Old Tay Bridge all the way round and went on to beat him ten lengths. On pulling up, Jack Anthony, who'd ridden Old Tay Bridge, asked me where I'd finished. "I've won," I replied. "Don't talk rubbish, I won," said Jack. He hadn't seen me, probably because he'd drunk a ginger beer bottle full of port before he went out to ride. He didn't know whether he'd won or not.'

*T. Leader (left) and G. Goswell (centre) in action at Ely Races
in the 1930s.*

Tuesday 14 April	£785	Three miles and four furlongs

1	Vaulx (C. Piggott)	11-12-1	Keith Piggott
2	Old Tay Bridge (F. Hartigan)	11-12-1	J. Anthony
3	Master Billie (P. Whitaker)	6-10-2	G. Turner

Winning owner Mr C. Piggott

16 ran.   Distances: 10l, 5l.   SP 8/1, 3/1 fav., 7/1.   Going good.

Vaulx, brown gelding by Benvenuto-Bairgen Breac

1926

The locally-trained mare Miss Balscadden was successful in the year's race. Owned and ridden by amateur rider David Thomas of Pyle near Bridgend, Miss Balscadden won what could be described as an eventful race.

Mr R. Havelock-Allan's Cashbox, who was a length or two in front, suddenly swerved as he came to the open ditch and pitched his rider, Mr Read, on top of the fence. Poor Mr Read laid on top of the obstacle, 'as though reclining on a couch', reported *The Western Mail*. Five horses somehow managed to negotiate the fence on the furthermost side away from the shaken Mr Read. Six others though were swerved away by their jockeys who feared that by attempting to jump the fence they would have put Mr Read in mortal danger.

Amateur rider David Thomas who won the 1926 Welsh Grand National on Miss Balscadden.

Miss Balscadden (no. 22), ridden by David Thomas, leads the field in the 1926 race.

While all this was going on Mr C.H. Horrell's Postino, the favourite on his fourth place in this year's Cheltenham Gold Cup, was racing into the lead and half-a-mile from home looked an assured winner. Mr Thomas though had other ideas and, under his strong driving, Miss Balscadden joined Postino at the last. In a terrific battle to the line the mare just managed to get home by a head.

Colonel J.H. Starkey's Vive, who carried top weight of 12st 7lb, under Roger Burford, was a further three lengths away third. Miss Balscadden, who was receiving three stone from Vive, was trained by Colonel Morgan Lindsay at Ystrad Mynach in the Valleys.

Morgan Lindsay trained many winners from his mountainside training ground. One person who remembered him was Mr W.J. Hearnden who was his stable lad from 1919 until 1927. He recalled, 'He was a real Christian and devout churchman and one of nature's rare gentlemen. He served in the South African War and the 1914-18 War in which he sadly lost three sons, all I think, in the space of three months.'

As for Miss Balscadden's rider, farmer David Thomas, a prominent rider in Welsh hunt-racing circles, later in the day he was to find himself up before the stewards. Willie Stott reported him on the grounds of foul riding after they had dead-heated for second place in the Cardiff Exchange Handicap. The stewards accepted Mr Thomas's explanation that, 'it was an error of judgement', but cautioned him to be more careful in future.

The famed Jack Anthony at Ely Races.

Some racing scribes thought Mr Thomas unlucky not to have won the 1924 Aintree National as the horse he was riding Pencoed was going really well when it came down two fences from the finish.

Tuesday 6 April	£785		Three miles and four furlongs
1 Miss Balscadden (Col. Morgan Lindsay)	7-9-7	Mr David Thomas	
2 Postino (A.H. Saxby)	6-11-12	G. Goswell	
3 Vive (A. Hastings)	11-12-7	R. Burford	

Winning owner Mr David Thomas

12 ran.   Distances: head, 3l.   SP 8/1, 3/1 fav., 10/1.   Going good.

Miss Balscadden, bay mare by Balscadden-Wilkinson

1927

Victory this year went to the oldest horse in the race, thirteen-year-old Snipe's Bridge, who to this day still holds the record as the race's oldest winner. Owned and trained by Captain R.M. Thompson of Cirencester, Snipe's Bridge, who was partnered by Willie Gurney, won by a length from Sir Ernest Wills's Animated, ridden by F. Sergeant. A further two lengths away came Colonel J.H. Sharkey's Vive, who carried top weight of 12st 7lb with regular pilot Roger Burford in the saddle.

There were fifteen runners and Postino, who had finished second the previous year, was made a 3/1 favourite. Mr H. Liddell's Silver Somme and Mr H.G. Selfridge's Misconduct, who were both fallers in this year's Aintree National finished down the field while Postino was pulled up. Gurney, a more than useful rider, who sometimes rode for Cardiff ship-owner Mr Ralph Morel, told *The Western Mail* reporter, 'It was a most comfortable ride and the horse jumped splendidly. I had been lying well up all the way. I jumped the last slightly in front and although Sergeant on Animated put in a strong challenge my mount had sufficient in reserve.'

Willie Gurney, not to be mistaken for Fred 'Darkie' Gurney, who was riding around the same time, was a particularly good hurdles jockey. He had been badly wounded during the Great War and had been awarded the Military Medal for conspicuous bravery and on demobilisation he was attached to Richard Payne's yard.

Tuesday 19 April	£785		Three miles and four furlongs
1 Snipe's Bridge (Capt. R.M. Thompson)	13-11-12	Willie Gurney	
2 Animated (G.S. de Winton)	7-9-11	F.W. Sergeant	
3 Vive (A. Hastings)	12-12-7	R. Burford	

15 ran.   Distances: 1l, 2l.   SP 6/1, 100-8, 100/8.
Fav. Postino 3/1 pulled up.
Snipe's Bridge, bay gelding by Dibsa-Faithful

1928

George Bowden, one of a select band of jockeys to have ridden in both the Derby and the Grand National, won this year's race on the 1926 winner Miss Balscadden who was now owned by Sir David Llewellyn. And no one was more delighted with the mare's success than her former owner Mr David Thomas who had sold her to the baronet for £1,000. They say backers have short memories and Miss Balscadden, who was carrying the same weight – 9st 7lb – as she had carried when winning the race two years previously, was the rank outsider of the fifteen runners. In fact, it was reported at the time that the leading Welsh bookmaker, Jimmy Jones, had laid her at odds of 100/1!

Bowden, who was a rare judge of pace, took command of the race a long way from home and won by a distance from Mr Fowler's Pop Ahead, ridden by F. Brookes, with Major Harold Werner's Toycup, ridden by Tommy Morgan, a bad third.

A smart young chaser called Knockirr was made the 3/1 favourite, but fell at the third fence. Bowden, aged twenty, who was riding his first winner over

George Bowden, who won the 1928 Welsh Grand National, seen here taking the water jump at Cardiff Races, c. 1930

Ely races was the place to be seen in the 1920s and 1930s.

fences, was the son of John Bowden, of Rectory Farm, Merthyr Dyfan, Barry. He had ridden his first winner for Colonel Morgan Lindsay on a horse called Breconian who was later to become a great favourite of Colonel Sir Harry Llewellyn.

Mrs Posy Lewis, of Llantwit Major, the first woman to be granted a licence to train under National Hunt rules recalled, 'George was a handsome and likeable fellow and he rode winners for my father, Ralph Morel, and later myself.' Bowden, who had served his apprenticeship with Yorkshire trainer Mr Golightly, died after a long illness at the East Glamorgan Hospital near Pontypridd in 1985.

Point-to-point stalwart Jack Thomas, of St Athan, recalled, 'I knew George well. We both schooled horses together in our younger days and I recall him riding a filly in the Derby which is a very rare thing indeed. It was called Stampede and was owned by Dr Sixsmith of Cowbridge and he used to ride the filly on his rounds. Anyway, it trailed in last.'

Jack Moloney, who rode the 1929 winner Monduco.

Tuesday 10 April	£785	Three miles and four furlongs

1	Miss Balscadden (Col. Morgan Lindsay)	9-9-7	George Bowden
2	Pop Ahead (S. Bennett)	10-10-7	F.J. Brookes
3	Toy Cup (A. Hastings)	7-9-13	T. Morgan

Winning owner Sir David Llewellyn

15 ran.   Distances: a distance.   bad.   SP 20/1, 6/1, 6/1.

Fav. Knockirr 3/1 fell.

Miss Balscadden, bay mare by Balscadden-Wilkinson

1929

A record twenty-one horses faced the starter for the 1929 Welsh Grand National and Mr Albert Bendon saw his purple and silver stars colours carried to victory by Monduco, a French-bred grey gelding, formerly known as Le Mont du Coq. Monduco, who was making his debut in this country, landed a huge gamble after being backed down from 8/1 to 2/1 favourite.

Ridden by Jack Maloney, Monduco scored by a length from Mr H.G. Selfridge's Ruddyman, partnered by Eric Brown, with Mr David Faber's Beech Martin, under Mr D. Royson, a further length away in third place.

Monduco, who had been laid out for this race, was trained in Wiltshire by that great racing character Percy Woodland. Born in 1884, Woodland rode his first winner in a steeplechase at Lingfield at the tender age of thirteen. He was equally as good on the flat as he was over-the-sticks and he is the only jockey to have ridden two Aintree National winners – Drumcree 1903, Covertcoat, 1913 – two Grand Steeplechase de Paris winners – Dandolo, 1904 and Canard, 1905 – and two French Derby winners Maintenon in 1906 and Or du Rhin in 1910. During the First World War he served in the RFC and was shot down and taken

Ely racecourse usually attracted large crowds, as can be seen in this picture taken in the 1930s.

Willie Stott

prisoner of war in Mesopotamia. Although he lived in France for some time before the war, where he trained many winners, it was at Cholderton, Wiltshire, that he set up his training establishment after it. He won the 1920 Lincolnshire Handicap with Furious but it was as a trainer of jumpers that he was more readily recognised.

Monduco's rider, Irishman Jack Maloney, had earlier in the year ridden the great Easter Hero to finish second in the Aintree National. A natural horseman, whose skill in the saddle earned him the admiration and respect of his fellow jockeys, Maloney was destined to finish second in the Aintree National on another two occasions. Mr Bendon was the owner of a very good horse called Wuffy which had won, among other races, the 1927 Ebor Handicap, but he preferred National Hunt to the flat racing game.

Tuesday 22 April	**£785**		**Three miles, four furlongs and fifty yards**
1 Monduco (Percy Woodland)		7-10-2	Jack Maloney
2 Ruddyman (Capt. J.B. Powell)		10-10-2	E. Brown
3 Beech-Martin (T. Rayson)		8-11-0	M.D. Rayson

Winning owner Mr Albert Bendon

21 ran.   Distances: 2l, ½l.   SP 2/1 fav., 100/7, 10/1.   Going good.

Monduco (late Le Mont du Coy), grey gelding by Isard II-Mary Adeane

1930

There was a close finish to this year's race with Mr E. Large's Boomlet, ridden by Carmarthen's Dudley Williams, getting home by a neck from Mr H. Gordon Selfridge's Ruddyman ridden by Willie Stott. A further ten lengths back in third place came Mr Frank Ambrose Clarke's Favourite Star, piloted by the American amateur rider Mr A.C. Bostwick who had ridden his first winner in this country at Hurst Park two years earlier.

Fred Williams, the popular starter and mine host of the Bear Hotel in Cowbridge and more importantly the father of Evan Williams, astride his hack, Gold Dust, a veteran of the Great War, got the field of eleven runners off to a good start. Boomlet, in a handy position throughout, took command of the race two fences out, but was strongly challenged at the last by Ruddyman. Williams riding for all his worth pulled Boomlet to the favoured inside rail, and in a desperate lunge to the line managed to catch the judge's eye.

Boomlet, who was winning for the third time this season, was trained by Ivor Anthony at Wroughton. The disappointment of the race was Mr Albert Bendon's Koko who had won the 1926 Cheltenham Gold Cup, but burdened with top weight of 12st 2lb he trotted home in last place. The winner, who carried 11st 6lb, started favourite at 9/4.

This was the first time the Tote operated at Ely Racecourse and backers of Boomlet who placed their money with the machine received a tote dividend of six shillings and sixpence for their two shillings (10p) stake which, as it happened, was the same amount they would have received had they backed their fancy at starting price.

The late Michael Williams, who was point-to-point correspondent of *The Sporting Life* for nearly fifty years, told me had the privilege of meeting Dudley Williams at the Portman Point-to-Point at Badbury Rings in the spring of 1965 and he recalled, 'Although Dudley never rode Golden Miller in a race, he rode work on him on numerous occasions, and on that other great horse Easter Hero; and naturally had plenty to say about both these horses. But, strangely enough, he had even more to say about Arkle. In fact he let loose a flood of eloquence. So, of course, I asked him the inevitable question, and received an illuminating reply. A toss of the coin, he said, would decide the difference between The Miller and Easter Hero. Both were better than Mill House, but neither was within 20 lengths of Arkle.'

Willie Stott was to die three years later following a car crash shortly after he had landed the 1933 Cheltenham Gold Cup and Champion Hurdle double with Golden Miller and Insurance respectively.

*Dudley Williams rode the 1933
winner Pebble Ridge and the 1930
winner Boomlet.*

Tuesday 22 April	£785	Three miles, four furlongs and fifty yards

1	Boomlet (Ivor Anthony)	10-11-6	Dudley Williams
2	Ruddyman (Capt. J.B. Powell)	11-10-9	W. Stott
3	Favourite Star (Ivor Anthony)	6-10-9	A. Bostwick

Winning owner Mr E. Large

11 ran.   Distances: 1l, 10l.   SP 9/4 fav., 8/1, 10/1.   Going good

Boomlet, chestnut gelding by Littleton-Boom

1931

Captain Roger 'Babe' Moseley, aged thirty-one, a well-known military rider on leave from the East, had earlier achieved the ambition of all soldier-riders when he won this year's Grand Military Steeplechase at Sandown Park on his own horse Slieve Grien. He also captured this year's Welsh Grand National on the 100/8 outsider Wise Don, owned by Miss M. Lark and trained by Richard Payne at Weedon.

Despite the heavy going, the race was run at a fast pace. The Irish challenger, Georgintown, was an early faller and rounding the bend to the straight Captain J.W. Bridge's Vinicole, ridden by Danny Morgan, headed The Black Fellow followed by Wise Don and the favourite Don Sancho and Quite Calm. Wise Don and Vinicole jumped the last together, but once on the flat Wise Don drew away to win by one-and-a-half lengths. Ralph Morel's Quite Calm, ridden by George Bowden, was a further fifteen lengths away in third place.

The names of some of the jockeys who finished among the also-rans will live for as long as the sport of steeplechasing exists. Dudley Williams, Billy Speck, Jack Maloney, Perry Harding, Billy Parvin and Eric Brown. Tough little Billy Speck, who was associated with that super horse Thomond II, sadly died four years later following a fall at Cheltenham in which he broke his back. Such was his popularity that his funeral procession was more than two miles long.

Perry Harding, one of only two amateur riders to have won the Champion Hurdle, was a brave and distinguished gentleman who was to become better

Ely Racecourse, home of the Welsh Grand National from 1895 to 1939.

Gerry Wilson.

known in military circles as Major-General Sir Reginald Peregrine Harding, D.S.O.

Wise Don's trainer Richard Payne was a good amateur rider in his day and rode a lot of winners. His younger brother Billy, who was champion jockey in 1911 when he rode 76 winners, won every race at Liverpool apart from the one that mattered most-the Grand National.

Tuesday 7 April	**£785**	**Three miles, four furlongs and fifty yards**
1 Wise Don (R. Payne)	a-10-5	Capt. Roger Moseley
2 Vinicole (I. Anthony)	7-9-7	D. Morgan
3 Quite Calm (Roberts)	7-9-7	G. Bowden

Winning owner Miss M. Lark

15 ran.   Distances: 1½l, 10l.   SP 100/8, 100/8, 100/6.   Fav. Don Sancho 5th.

Going heavy.

Wise Don, brown gelding by Lorenzo-Puzzle

1932

Mrs Anthony Belville's six-year-old mare Miss Gaynus, ridden by Gerry Wilson and trained by J.L. 'Sonny' Hall at Ferny Compton, was an easy winner of this year's race. Jumping the last fence alongside Silver Grail, partnered by Billy Parvin, Miss Gaynus drew clear on the run-in to win by fifteen lengths. Wg Cdr W. Reed's The Black Fellow, who carried top weight of 12st 3lb, under Gerry Goswell, finished a bad third.

Of the ten starters these were the only finishers. Mrs Anthony Belville, later the Hon. Mrs Audrey Playdell-Bouverie, reminisced, 'The going was very deep. I bought Miss Gaynus in Ireland at Goffs Sales as an unbroken two or it might have been three-year-old and she cost not more than £100. I hunted her with the Bicester and although she was only about 15.2 hands high she won a few sellers and we realised she had potential. Gerry (Wilson) always rode her. When I was hunting her I seemed easily to pass most of the horses out.' She continued, 'I got Fred Withington who trained in Bicester country to give her a few gallops and schools and she showed promise again. I then sent her to Sonny (Hall).'

Although Gerry Wilson was the champion jockey his great days were still ahead of him. In 1934 he won the Cheltenham Gold Cup and the Grand National on the legendary Golden Miller. He was also successful in the 1935 Cheltenham Gold Cup on The Miller and he rode Lion Courage to victory in the 1934 Champion Hurdle. One of the outstanding National Hunt jockeys of his time, Wilson won the National Hunt jockeys' championship a then record-breaking seven times between 1932 and 1941. He came into racing in a very modest way riding anything that was offered to him at small meetings. He rode many winners for 'Sonny' Hall and it wasn't long after that other owners and trainers were seeking his services. When he hung up his riding boots to become a trainer he saddled the 1945 Champion Hurdle winner Brains Trust, but he never enjoyed the success that he had when he was riding.

Tuesday 29 March	£605		Three miles, four furlongs and fifty yards
1 Miss Gaynus (J.L. Hall)	6-11-0	Gerry Wilson	
2 Silver Grail (W.J. Powell)	6-11-8	W. Parvin	
3 The Black Fellow (W. Read)	8-12-3	G. Goswell	

Winning owner Mrs A. Belville

15 ran.   Distances: 15l. bad.   SP 6/1, 7/1, 4/1.   Fav. Quite Calm 3/1 fell.

Going heavy.

Miss Gaynus, bay mare by Cygnus-Gay Spanker

1933

This was the year that Dudley Williams won the Aintree National on Frank Ambrose Clark's Kellsboro' Jack. Kellsboro' Jack beat Major Noel Furlong's Really True by three lengths and in this year's Welsh equivalent, Dudley Williams, riding Lord Glanely's Pebble Ridge, scored by the same distance from Mr Edward Thomas Tyrwhitt Drake's Holmes, ridden by C. Beechener, after taking up the running two fences from the finish.

Lord Inchcape's Annandale, who headed the handicap, finished the same distance away in third place with Danny Morgan in the saddle. Harry Llewellyn, later Colonel Sir Harry Llewellyn, on his own horse Silver Grail was fourth. Many years later he recalled, 'The hard ground did not suit Silver Grail and he hit almost every fence. He was shin-sore and foot-sore for days afterwards. I remember the race caused quite a sensation as Pebble Ridge had finished last in all his previous races, yet he was backed down to 6/4 favourite!'

West Walian Dudley Williams on Kellsboro' Jack, winner of the Aintree Grand National in 1933.

Lord Glanely had strong ties with Cardiff. Some years earlier, as plain William James Tatem, he started work as a clerk in a shipping office at Cardiff Docks and worked so hard that by 1909 he was able to form his own company. Affectionately known to the racing public as 'Old Guts and Gaiters', Lord Glanely saw his famous racing colours carried to success in the 2000 Guineas (Columbo 1934), 1000 Guineas (Dancing Time 1941), Derby (Grand Parade 1919), Oaks (Rose of England 1930) and St Leger (Singapore 1930 and Chumleigh 1937).

Dudley Williams was one of a select band of Welshmen who dominated the National Hunt racing scene between the wars. He had been unlucky not to have won the 1930 Aintree National as the horse he was riding, Sir Lindsay, nearly fell at the last causing him to lose both stirrups. Despite this handicap, Sir Lindsay finished a close third to Shaun Goilin and Melleray's Belle beaten a neck and one-and-a-half lengths in one of the tightest finishes the race had ever produced.

It was said of Dudley that no jockey had ever ridden the Aintree course with greater skill or courage. Besides the Aintree National Dudley also won the Stanley Chase and Grand Sefton which were then Aintree's other big steeple-chase events. He was leading jockey in 1934 when he had a bad fall at Hurst Park and never rode again. In 1940 he put his talents and skills to other uses and began training at Beckhampton. From this famous racing centre he sent out many winners and most of them were ridden by his great friend Gordon (later Sir Gordon) Richards. He always insisted that Sir Gordon, being born in Shropshire, was a Welshman. When I had the honour of meeting Sir Gordon at a press luncheon at Chepstow Racecourse a couple of years before he died I reminded him of this and although he agreed that Richards was a Welsh name, he didn't quite agree to being Welsh!

Sadly, Dudley ended his days in Yeovil Hospital and died soon after having his right leg amputated. He phoned me shortly before he died and during our conversation he revealed that at one time he was offered a large sum to write his autobiography. What a great loss to racing that he never got around to writing it.

Tuesday 18 April	£488	Three miles, four furlongs and fifty yards
1 Pebble Ridge (I. Anthony)	8-10-11	Dudley Williams
2 Holmes (C. Beechener)	13-11-4	C. Beechener
3 Annadale (Maj. F.W. Barrett)	11-12-0	D. Morgan

Winning owner Lord Glanely

9 ran.   Distances 3l, 3l.   SP 6/4 fav., 7/1, 8/1.   Going good.

Pebble Ridge, brown gelding by Westward Ho-Little Mable

1934

The royal blue and primrose racing colours of James Voase Rank were to prove successful in five of the six remaining Welsh Grand Nationals that were run at Cardiff's Ely Racecourse. One of steeplechasing's greatest patrons, Mr Rank owned a number of fine jumpers. These included Prince Regent who was to win the 1946 Cheltenham Gold Cup and who was rated not that far behind the mighty Arkle by his trainer Tom Dreaper. But Mr Rank's nine-year-old Dream Ship, ridden by Jack Fawcus, could be considered a lucky winner of this year's race as Major Noel Furlong's Really True had the race all sewn up approaching the last when he suddenly swerved off the track crashing into some hurdles nearby.

Really True's jockey, Frank Furlong, had no chance as it transpired that his mount's bridle had snapped as he came to jump the last. This left Dream Ship

Jack Fawcus, who rode four Welsh Grand National winners, on the 1931 Aintree Grand National winner Grakle.

Frank Furlong.

to finish four lengths ahead of Mr J. Snow's Delaneige, ridden by Jack Moloney, who had been runner-up to Golden Miller in this year's Aintree National . The same distance away in third place came Mr A. Bazley's Broodwas with Eric Brown in the saddle.

Dream Ship, as we shall see, was the first of four Welsh Grand National winners to be trained by Welshman Gwyn Evans at Lewes. He also saddled three Scottish Grand National winners in Southern Hero (1934 & 1936) and Young Mischief (1938). And had he not been tragically killed in a car crash in 1938, at the age of forty-six, would have saddled Lacatoi who was to win the race a record-breaking three times.

Frank Furlong, who had been second on Really True in the 1933 Aintree National was successful on Reynoldstown in the 1935 race. When war broke out in 1939 he joined the Fleet Air Arm and was killed returning from a reconnaissance flight in 1944 at the early age of thirty-four.

Tuesday 3 April	£488	Three miles, four furlongs and fifty yards
1 Dream Ship (G. Evans)	8-11-7	Jack Fawcus
2 Delaneige (G. Beeby)	9-12-3	J. Moloney
3 Broadwas (R. Bennett)	7-10-7	E. Brown

Winning owner Mr J.V. Rank
10 ran.   4l, 4l.   SP 4/1, 7/4 fav., 8/1.   Going good.
Dream Ship, bay gelding by Argossy-Sweet Dream

1935

There were forty-eight entries for the 1935 Welsh Grand National and twelve of them went to post. These twelve included the previous year's winner Dream Ship. Joint-favourites were Lacatoi and Avenger but it was the bottom-weighted Ego who made all the early running.

A mile from home, Jack Fawcus on little Lacatoi moved up fast and entering the straight deprived Major-General William S. Anthony's Aureate Earth of the lead. Aureate Earth, a beaten horse, fell at the last and Lacatoi, shaking off the challenge of Fred Rimell on Mrs Violet Mundy's Avenger, scored by one-and-a-half lengths.

Ego, under Mr J. Kirton, finished third a further three lengths away. Lacatoi giving owner Mr Rank and trainer Gwyn Evans their second success in the race. Mr Rank's second string Dream Ship finished way back in sixth place. Fred Rimell recalling the race many years later said that the shrewd Fawcus had walked the course beforehand and found some good going where sheep had been grazing and naturally during the race he picked the better ground.

Jack Fawcus, who was amateur champion in 1931/2, rode a lot for Mr Rank. On Mr Rank's Southern Hero he won the Scottish Grand National three times in 1934, 1936 and 1939. Other big races he won included the Imperial Cup, National Hunt Chase and the Liverpool Hurdle. The years he spent as a prisoner of war during the Second World War left their mark on the health of Captain John Fawcus who took out a trainer's licence in 1946. The best horse he ever trained was probably Cool Customer who won 19 races including the Great Yorkshire. He also saddled the 1958 Scottish Grand National winner Game Field. Sadly, he was killed in a motor car accident on his way to Uttoxeter races in May 1967. His son Charles Fawcus rode as an amateur and later was a racing journalist writing under the *nom de plume* Newsboy for the *Daily Mirror*.

Tuesday 23 April	£535	Three miles, four furlongs and fifty yards

1	Lacatoi (G. Evans)	7-10-8	Jack Fawcus
2	Avenger (D. Harrison)	6-11-12	T.F. Rimell
3	Ego (Capt. M. Lindsay)	8-9-8	Mr J. Kirton

Winning owner Mr J.V. Rank

12 ran.   Distances: 1½l, 3l.   SP 4/1 jt. fav., 4/1 jt. fav., 8/1.   Going good.

Lacatoi, by Yutoi-Cider

1936

The attendance at Ely Racecourse for the 1936 Welsh Grand National was reported to have been the highest for years. This was no doubt brought about by the appearance of the legendary Golden Miller, already a winner of an unprecedented five Cheltenham Gold Cups and a Grand National. When he was paraded before the start, Golden Miller looked a picture, and despite the fact that he shouldered top weight of 12st 7lb the bookmakers made him a 4/6 odds-on favourite.

'At the first open ditch by the stands no fewer than four horses came to grief', reported *The Western Mail*. These were Dream Ship, Swallow Hawk, Lazy Boots and Comedian. According to Swallow Hawk's rider, Tim Hamey, a dog ran right across the ditch causing the chaos that brought the four horses down. For a great part of the journey, the Northern-trained horse, Tommy Tittlemouse, led the remaining runners, but was done for second time around.

Mr Frank Ambrose Clark leads in his 1936 Welsh Grand National winner Sorley Boy. When Sorley Boy died, he was buried on the summit of one of the foothills of the Adirondacks.

Fred Williams, the popular starter, leading the parade. He is followed by his son Evan on Golden Miller.

Danny Morgan on Mr Frank Ambrose Clark's Sorley Boy took over the lead until four fences from home when he was joined by Evan Williams on the mighty 'Miller'. Morgan, knowing he had 23lb less to carry than Golden Miller, kicked on with the result that Miss Dorothy Paget's famed steeplechaser could find no extra. Williams, realising he couldn't win, eased his mount allowing Mr Louis Stoddard riding his own horse Free Wheeler, who was receiving a hefty 33lb, to gain second place.

The official distances were one length and three lengths. Those racegoers who backed Golden Miller for a place on the tote were rewarded with odds of more than 2/1 against. Amazingly, the tote paid a dividend of six shillings and threepence to a two-shilling stake!

Sorley Boy, a ten-year-old brown gelding by Cottage-Maura Kishaun, was trained by Ivor Anthony at Wroughton in Swindon. Although Sorley Boy's rider, Danny Morgan, was never fortunate to win the Aintree National he won three Scottish Grand Nationals with Annandale (1931), Kellsboro' Jack (1935) and Young Mischief (1938). He also won two Champion Hurdles with Chenango (1934) and National Spirit (1947) and in 1938 he won the Cheltenham Gold Cup on Morse Code. Other big races that went his way included the Champion Chase (on three occasions), the Grand Sefton and The Liverpool Hurdle. As a trainer, this popular little Irishman saddled the 1959 Cheltenham Gold Cup winner Roddy Owen.

Golden Miller, which came third in the 1936 race.

Tuesday 14 April   **£535**   **Three miles, four furlongs and fifty yards**

1	Sorley Boy (I. Anthony)	10-10-12	Danny Morgan
2	Free Wheeler (I. Anthony)	6-10-5	Mr L. Stoddard
3	Golden Miller (O. Anthony)	9-12-7	E. Williams

Winning owner Mr F.A. Clark

11 ran.   Distances: 1l, 3l.   SP 8/1, 10/1, 4/6 fav.   Going good.

Sorley Boy, brown gelding by Cottage-Maura Kishaun

1937

Eighty-one runners for the six races at Ely Racecourse on Easter Tuesday, 1937, constituted a record for the racetrack. The thirteen horses for this year's Welsh Grand National included the previous year's winner Sorley Boy and Lacatoi who had been successful in 1935.

After the first circuit the field was reduced to six runners with Mrs Violet Mundy's Custom House, under Fred Rimell, cutting out the lead. Keen Blade, Hypericum, Bryan O'Linn and La Touche had all fallen. Torrish had refused and Tapinios and Dinna Fear had pulled up!

Entering the straight, Jack Fawcus on the 2/1 favourite Lacatoi challenged Custom House and an exhilarating race between these two ensued for the rest of the journey. At the last there was nothing in it, but once on the flat the game little Lacatoi drew away to win by two-and-a-half lengths. Mr A. Pilkington's Pencralk, ridden by George Archibald, was a further five lengths away in third place. Spionard was fourth, Blaze was fifth and Sorley Boy trailed in sixth and last.

An objection to the winner, by the rider of the runner-up, on the ground of crossing, was overruled. Custom House's owner, Mrs Violet Mundy, was known in racing circles as 'Hellcat Mundy' because of her blunt and outspoken manner. She was a great supporter of Welsh racing and point-to-pointing and occasionally acted

Gwyn Evans, who trained four Welsh Grand National winners, seen winning a point-to-point race in west Wales.

Harry Llewellyn being led in after winning on China Sea at Ely Races in 1937.

as a steward at point-to-points. She had horses in training with David Harrison and later with Fred Rimell's father Tom Rimell. A grey horse called Henri's Choice proved just as much an attraction to visitors at the track as did Lacatoi. For Henri's Choice, who won the Cardiff Exchange Handicap Hurdle, had two years previously broken his neck in a fall at Liverpool. His life was saved by the skill of veterinary surgeons and fully recovering from his remarkable operation, Henri's Choice went on to win several races.

Tuesday 30 March	£535	Three miles, four furlongs and fifty yards

1	Lacatoi (G. Evans)	9-10-5	Jack Fawcus
2	Custom House (T.R. Rimell)	6-10-13	T.F. Rimell
3	Pencraik (Capt. K. Goode)	10-9-13	G. Archibald

Winning owner Mr J.V. Rank

13 ran.   Distances: 2½l, 5l.   SP 2/1 fav., 3/1, 100/8.   Going good.

Lacatoi, by Yutoi-Cider

1938

Of the thirty-six entries for the 1938 Welsh Grand National just three of them – Mr J.V. Rank's Timber Wolf, Mr D. Marshall's Black Hawk and Captain Blake's Epiphanes – lined up for the start. Even so the smallest field in the history of the race – the going was on the hard side – produced a stirring finish with the grey Timber Wolf, ridden by seventeen-year-old Bruce Hobbs, holding on by a length from Danny Morgan's mount Black Hawk, after being three lengths down at the last fence. In fact, Black Hawk made a great race of it being in close attendance of the favourite throughout the whole three-and-a-half miles. Epiphanes, partnered by Mr H. Applin, on the other hand, was never in the hunt and finished a distant third.

Bruce Hobbs, who had earlier made turf history by being the youngest rider ever to win the Aintree National on Battleship, told me that he is of Welsh extraction his grandfather having been born in Cardiff. He remembered Timber Wolf making a bad mistake at the water jump when Black Hawk was alongside and said, 'The horse Danny Morgan rode I had ridden previously in the Scottish Grand National when he started favourite and ran badly. They asked me to ride him at Cardiff but I declined in favour of Timber Wolf.'

Born in America, the son of National Hunt trainer Reg Hobbs, it was appropriate that this year he also won the Cedarhurst Grand National in the United States. During the Second World War he was made a captain in the Queen's Own Yorkshire Dragoons and won the Military Cross. He later trained on the flat with great success.

Tuesday 19 April	£560	Three miles, four furlongs and fifty yards
1 Timber Wolf (G. Evans)	10-11-3	Bruce Hobbs
2 Black Hawk (J. Goldsmith)	7-11-5	D. Morgan
3 Epiphanes (A.J. Bridgman)	6-9-8	Mr H. Applin

Winning owner Mr J.V. Rank

3 ran.   Distances: 1l, a distance.   SP 10/11 fav., 11/8, 6/1.   Going firm.

Timber Wolf, by Werewolf

1939

There were eleven starters for the last Welsh Grand National to be staged at Cardiff. The race provided a grand tussle between the local mare, Major E.C. Morel's Waving Star, ridden by Alec Marsh, and Mr J.V. Rank's dual winner Lacatoi, ridden as usual by Jack Fawcus.

No story of Ely Racecourse or the Welsh Grand National could be complete without reference to the Morel family. Their black, red and white colours, taken from the family shipping line, were immensely popular with racegoers.

It looked as though Waving Star would record a local victory as she went half-a-dozen or so lengths clear after jumping the last. But Fawcus somehow conjured up a late run on Lacatoi to get up in the last few yards to win by the shortest of short heads. Lady Curre's Dinton Lad, ridden by Tommy Isaac, was

Jack Fawcus on Lacatoi being led in by Mrs James V. Rank.

Lacatoi wins the Welsh Grand National for a third time in 1939.

two lengths back in third. Major Morel's neice, Posy Morel, as Mrs G.R. Lewis, redressed the balance, albeit some years later, by training Limonali to win in 1959 and 1961. Mrs Lewis, recalling the race to Pat Lucas in *Fifty Years of Racing at Chepstow Racecourse*, said, 'She was six or seven lengths clear and suddenly, it was all over. She was beaten by a short head. We found out afterwards that she had cricked her back, but it was all very disappointing for my uncle.'

Alec Marsh, who rode Waving Star, was a very good amateur rider who had won the Cheltenham Foxhunters on Empire Night in 1935 and in 1936 on Herod Bridge. He rode a total of 163 winners and these included 21 on the Flat. Between 1953-72 he was appointed a Jockey Club starter.

Tuesday 11 April	**£535**	**Three miles, four furlongs and fifty yards**
1 Lacatoi (H.A. Brown)	11-10-11	Jack Fawcus
2 Waving Star (Maj. E.C. Morel)	7-11-1	Mr A. Marsh
3 Dinton Lad (J. Norris)	7-11-6	T. Isaac

Winning owner Mr J.V. Rank

11 ran.   Distances: short head, 2l.   SP 7/4 fav., 8/1, 8/1.   Going good.

Lacatoi, by Yutoi-Cider.

MEMORIES OF ELY RACECOURSE

Many people had fond memories of Ely racecourse. Welshman Evan Williams set an unusual record when on Easter Monday 1933 he rode the first winner, Mr Ghandi, as an amateur rider and the last, Vive L'Amour, as a professional jockey.

Mr Douglas Leslie whose father Colonel David Leslie was the official handicapper there for a number of years recalled:

> My father and I always stayed with Mr C.C. Williams at Llanrumney Hall, St Mellons, Cardiff (now a public house on a large council estate) Squire Williams had what was known to us as 'The Hut', which was a wooden shed fitted out to accommodate friends for a superb picnic lunch with all the refreshments that anyone could ever ask for. Here one met the Hon. Mrs Violet Mundy who was one of the nicest people imaginable. Her colours were of a small harlequin pattern.
>
> One unforgettable character was Mr David Harrison who trained at Tenby. A big square-shouldered fellow with a gruff voice. He trained for many of the South Wales owners and rode himself in his earlier days. His horses were ridden by the brothers Jack and Ivor Anthony and F.B. Rees. He also had a lad called Duggan who rode his not-so-good-uns, and some hairy rides the poor chap used to get too, I remember.
>
> All the jumping trainers were to be found in Squire Williams's hut, Max Barthropp, Arthur Stubbs, Miles Thompson and Bay Powell to name a few. Then, of course, there was Mr R.H. 'Bobby' Williams, Joint Master of the Glamorgan Hunt, Mr Claude Williams, old Captain Hastings Clay, and Johnny Clay the famous cricketer, Mr and Mrs Harbor Homfray from the Glamorgan Hunt, and their daughter Anne, later Lady Boothby.
>
> I can also remember Ben Warner the well-known punter of those days, Tommy Andrews who won the Powderhall Professional Sprint, Ted Arnold the England and Worcestershire cricketer, and Jimmy Wilde the famous boxer. Folk from every conceivable walk of life were welcome in 'The Hut' and a couple of days racing at Cardiff were glorious fun with never a dull moment.

Former Irish jockey H.J. Delmege of County Tipperary claims that Cardiff's Ely Racecourse was the first racecourse where crash helmets were worn: 'I rode Navan Boy at the October 1923 meeting and we had to wear helmets. They were neat and weighed only a few ounces, nothing like the piss pots worn now which remind me of the knights of old jousting.'

*Mrs Violet Mundy, a regular at Ely Races. (Photograph
courtesy of Mrs C.C. Williams)*

Owen Anthony on the gallops.

Ely Racecourse was dubbed 'The Ascot of Wales'.

Amateur rider David Thomas, who won the 1926 Welsh Grand National on Miss Balscadden.

Arthur Byrd said:

From the age of twelve, and after when I left school, I worked on the racecourse for a number of years in the weighing room where I helped to dispense drinks to the owners, trainers and jockeys, who always had a stiff drink before going out to face the hazards of the profession.

The paddock and weighing room were unique in racing as they were situated not on the stands side but on the cheap enclosure, and the owners and trainers had to walk from the stands side to view the horses in the parade ring.

I saw all the well-known jockeys and owners of the time: the Anthony and Rees brothers, Willie Stott and the then-amateur rider Harry Llewellyn. Then there was Lord Glanely and the leading bookmaker Jimmy Jones from Newport who owned Black Isle, Lady Gay and Stow Hill. He also owned a greyhound which beat the legendary Mick the Miller in a match at Cardiff's Sloper Road Greyhound Stadium.

Bob Sparkes remembered standing on Ely Bridge on his way home from Sunday School and watching the horses arrive by train: 'It was a most colourful sight to see the horses being led out of the carriages and walked to the racecourse stables at the back of Mill Road. The atmosphere was electric, just like a carnival or fun fair.'

For George Holland, Cardiff race days meant more pocket money: 'After racing, a gang of us boys would descend on the track and collect all the empty beer bottles and take them back for the deposit money, which was more than welcome in those days.'

Bookmaker Bill White recalled: 'In the 1930s my beginnings as a bookmaker got off to a disastrous start. I was eighteen and it was the first time for me to stand as a bookmaker on the racecourse. It was the two-day Easter Bank Holiday meeting and most of the races were won by either the first or second favourites which meant I paid out much more money than what I took.'

Mr White also remembered visiting Ely Racecourse as a young boy with his father: 'As we walked to the entrance of the track the poor inmates of the

Player's cigarette card depicting L.B. Rees taking a tumble.

From left to right: Evan Williams, Fred Williams, Mrs Aubrey Hastings and Tommy Wilton-Pye, clerk of the course.

mental hospital would be leaning over the hospital wall begging for coppers. One of these unfortunates we got to know quite well. Little Freddie we called him, and my father would throw him a couple of shillings to catch.'

One man who worked at Ely Racecourse as a young boy was Mr A.E. Pursey and he recalled: 'After we had finished building the fences, the Clerk of the Course, Mr Tommy Wilton-Pye, who was a very nice man, used to take the lads for a drink in the White Lion. Unfortunately, however, I was only sixteen so had to wait outside.'

The late Fulke Walwyn, who needs no introduction, reminisced: 'I had my first ride under National Hunt rules at Cardiff, and luckily for me it turned out to be a winner. The horse's name was Alpine Hut and I won a two-mile novice chase on him. He turned out to be a very useful horse and won a lot of races, which helped me along. Cardiff was a good course and it is such a pity that most of these meetings have now gone.'

William Heariden, stableman to Colonel Morgan Lindsay for many years and a former jockey himself, wrote:

> We had many winners at Ely from our stables in Ystrad Mynach. Breconian, Tarriddle and Miss Balscadden to name just a few. The last named won the Welsh Grand National there on two occasions. When she pulled off the double in 1928 she was ridden by my great friend George Bowden, who was Colonel Morgan Lindsay's stable jockey at the time. To me Ely was a lovely course, a left-handed one with an uphill gradient on the far side under the Ely Woods with well-built fences.

1948

With the closure of Ely Racecourse in 1939 the first post-war Welsh Grand National was to have taken place at Newport's Caerleon Racecourse in 1947. However, owing to the course being waterlogged it would be 1948 before the race was revived. Occasional race meetings had been held at Newport's Caerleon Racecourse since 1845 but thanks to the support of the Llangibby and Lord Tredegar hunts in the late 1890s more meetings on a regular basis were to take place there.

Bayles' book *The Racecourses of Great Britain and Ireland* published around 1906 was full of praise for the track, 'No meeting could be better controlled, and unlimited praise is due to its Management, because it is self evident that every energy is devoted to the comfort and consideration of its patrons, for it can be annually recognised that improvements are constantly being made. An excellent example for others who have the subject of sporting

Mrs 'Hellcat' Violet Mundy leading in her horse Teme Water at Newport, Caerleon Races.

Paddock scene, Caerleon, Newport races.

form uppermost. There are two courses, one for chases and one for hurdle races, both with a running line right handed. The shape takes an outline of a cornered square. The run-in is 400 yards. The fences are birch, well built and to proper size. The turf is very good going, and well drained. The conformation is nicely undulating. Free stabling. Hotels at Caerleon and Newport.'

Mr F.L. Vickerman's Bora's Cottage was successful in the only Welsh Grand National held at Newport. Ten-year-old Bora's Cottage was by that famous sire of steeplechasers Cottage who also sired this year's Aintree National winner Sheila's Cottage. Ridden by Eddie Reavey, Bora's Cottage scored by ten lengths from Mrs May Harvey's Royal Mint with Salutation a further six lengths away in third place.

Mrs Jocelyn Reavey, who was a 'stable lad' when girls were a rarity in those days recalled, 'My late husband Eddie rode the first big winner ever trained by Ryan Price. He rode lots of winners for the Captain but this win was one that was never forgotten by either of them.' Winning the Welsh Grand National was some little consolation for poor Eddie Reavey. In this year's Aintree National he had taken a wrong turn after jumping the penultimate fence when clear on the 100/1 chance Zahia and this mishap almost certainly cost him the race.

Bora's Cottage's trainer, the controversial Captain Ryan Price, a former leading point-to-point rider in the 1930s, went on to win every race worth winning over-the-sticks and a few more on the Flat as well and was leading trainer on four occasions. Mr Vickerman was best known as the owner of the immortal Cottage Rake – also by Cottage – who had won three successive Cheltenham Gold Cups.

Sadly, Newport Racecourse which was in dire straits financially staged its final meeting a month later. It was at Newport in 1924 that an objection to Simon's Glory the winner of the Tredegar Handicap Hurdle was probably unique in the history of the turf. The objection raised was that instead of covering the stipulated distance of two-and-a-half miles the horses completed the two-and-three-quarter miles course. After much deliberation the stewards declared the race void and fined the clerk of the course £25!

Tuesday 30 March	£1,030	Three miles, four furlongs and 150 yards
1 Bora's Cottage (H.R. Price)	10-10-2	Eddie Reavey
2 Royal Mount (J. Powell)	9-11-2	P. Doyle
3 Salutation (C. Birch)	7-10-5	Mr J. Spencer

Winning owner Mr F.L. Vickerman

16 ran.   Distances 10l, 6l, a distance.   SP 100/8, 5/2 fav., 100/7.

Bora's Cottage, bay gelding by Cottage-Bora

1949

Few racecourses are surrounded by such beautiful countryside as can be seen at Chepstow's Piercefield Park. Little wonder that when the racecourse was opened in 1926, when 20,000 racegoers attended the inaugural flat race meeting, it was dubbed 'The Glorious Goodwood of the West'.

Not far from the banks of the River Wye, it is indeed a glorious and delightful racecourse. Since the first rain-washed National Hunt fixture of 1927 Chepstow has come a long way. And it is all thanks to those pioneering stalwarts on the initial board of directors Sir David Hughes Morgan, Sir Henry Webb the Lords Glanely, Tredegar, Queensborough and Messrs W.R. Lysaght, R.E. Morel, Henry Hastings Clay, R. Huggett, Hwfa Williams and G.L.B. Francis.

Although dogged by serious financial difficulties in the early years, these imaginative gentlemen with the help of their shareholders and a understanding bank manager, saw to it that Chepstow Racecourse survived at a time when neighbouring tracks at Tenby. Monmouth, Cardiff and Newport were all closing their gates. And this was long before the Severn Bridge made Chepstow accessible to racegoers from all parts of the country.

Stable lad David Owens leading in the 1949 Welsh Grand National Winner, Fighting Line.

Fighting Line and Dick Francis jump the last in the 1949 Welsh Grand National.

After the Second World War, and the closure of the nearby Caerleon course, the Welsh Grand National came to Chepstow in 1949 and it was most appropriate that the first running of the race was won by a Welshman – Dick Francis. Riding Mrs C.A. Hall-Hall's Fighting Line he had the ten-year-old gelding in a handy position from the start and taking the lead at the thirteenth fence went on to win by eight lengths from the favourite Old Mortality ridden by Bob Turnell. A further two lengths away came the third horse the top weighted Cavaliero ridden by Paddy Doyle. Having finished second on Roimond in the Aintree race, this win was a consolation prize for Francis.

Fighting Line, by His Reverence out of Beline, was bought by his owner at the Newmarket Autumn Sales for 550 guineas and won fourteen races and more than £6,000 in prize money for her. A former RAF pilot, who went on to become a best-selling author of racing novels, Francis rode for George Owen after the war as an amateur with considerable success. He became champion jockey in 1953/4 when he rode 76 winners.

He recounted, 'I was born and bred in Pembrokeshire, although I did move from there with my family at quite a young age. Before moving to Berkshire, my father Vincent Francis had been stable jockey to Lort Phillips, whose stables were situated at Lawrenny, and he rode the same time as the Anthony brothers, and in the early days of the Rees brothers. Indeed my father's father, my grandfather, lived next door to Brychan Rees, a veterinary surgeon who attended the horses of David Harrison the Tenby trainer.'

*Dan Morgan, who rode in
ten Grand Nationals.*

Tuesday 19 April	**£1,015**	**Three miles and six furlongs**

1 Fighting Line (K. Cundell)   10-10-9   Dick Francis
2 Old Mortality (T.F. Rimell)   7-11-8   R. Turnell
3 Cavaliero (J. Powell)   8-12-2   P. Doyle

Winning owner Mrs C.A. Hall-Hall

15 ran.   Distances: 8l, 2l, 1½l.   SP 7/1, 9/4 fav., 7/1.   Going good.

Fighting Line, bay gelding by His Reverence-Beline

1950

There were fifty-nine entries for this year's race, but only twelve of them went to post. Monmouthshire's Alf Mullins, who had started his race-riding career in point-to-points in the 1930s, captured this year's race on Sir Arthur Pilkington's twelve-year-old Gallery who to this day remains the oldest winner of the race since it has been staged at Chepstow. Snipe's Bridge who won at Cardiff in 1927 was thirteen.

Gallery, trained by William Rippon Bissill at Aslockton, Nottinghamshire, came home five lengths clear of Land Fort ridden by Bob Turnell who was later to train the 1972 winner Charlie H. Battling Pendulas was third and Deelish fourth. George Bowden, who had won on Miss Balscadden back in 1928, finished among the also-rans on Morning Star II and is the only rider to have ridden in the race before and after the Second World War. The previous year's winner Fighting Line blotted his copybook by refusing under Dick Francis. Alf Mullins, in the words of Michael Scudamore was, 'A very brave and hard jockey.'

There cannot be too many instances in racing of two brothers riding a dead-heat, but this is what happened at the Llangibby Point-To-Point in 1933 when Alf aboard Juno dead-heated with his brother Jack on Irish Melody. Alf got to ride a lot of moderate horses but, as we shall see, he was to go down in the history books as the first rider to win the Chepstow Welsh Grand National on two occasions.

One celebrated jockey who finished down the field that day was Jack Dowdeswell, champion jockey in 1946/47. They didn't come tougher than Jack who during his riding career broke fifty-two different bones in his body and who once had an arm torn clean out of its socket. On one occasion, after a race riding accident, he had to have stitches in his penis. On returning to the weighing room his fellow jockeys asked him how many stitches he had to have and he told them nine. To which they replied, 'Bragging again!' Gallery's trainer Mr Bissill, who had ridden as an amateur before the war, had won the 1937 Scottish Grand National with Right 'Un.

Tuesday 11 April	£1,025		Three miles and six furlongs
1 Gallery (W. Bissill)		12-10-8	Alf Mullins
2 Land Fort (T.F. Rimell)		6-10-9	R. Turnell
3 Battling Pendulas (J. Beary)		11-10-9	G. Kelly

Winning owner Sir Arthur Pilkington

12 ran.   Distances: 5l, 8l, 8l.   SP 7/2, 11/4 fav., 8/1.   Going good.

Gallery, bay gelding by Winalot-Nunnery

1951

Despite the recent heavy rain, the weather was fine and the going on the good side for the 1951 renewal of the Welsh Grand National. Middleham trainer Neville Crump saw his Skyreholme, partnered by Arthur Thompson, or A.P. Thompson as he was more popularly known, get up by a head to beat the 1949 winner Fighting Line ridden by Charlie Smithers. However, many racegoers thought that Fighting Line should have been judged the winner so close was the finish. A further twenty lengths back in third place came Brown Hall partnered by the champion jockey Tim Molony.

Skyreholme, who won three hurdle races and four steeplechases during his racing career, raced for two more seasons, but never won again. Arthur Thompson, who always liked to make all the running on his mounts, came to Britain in the 1930s and had ridden chiefly for Harry Peacock. He joined the army when war was declared and was captured in France but he managed to escape on a stolen bicycle. Obviously he couldn't find a horse! After the war, he took up his riding career again and rode two Aintree National winners Sheila's Cottage (1948) and Teal (1952). He returned to Ireland in 1956 and took out a trainer's licence, but later took up farming. He died in 1988 aged seventy-one. Jack Douglas, headman at Neville Crump's yard, said, 'We were the best of friends for forty years and he was one of the best men across country since the war and was certainly the bravest.'

Neville Crump trained three Aintree National winners Sheila's Cottage, Teal and the 1960 winner Merryman II. He also saddled three Scottish Grand National winners Wot No Sun (1949), Merryman II (1959) and Acturus (1968).

Saturday 14 April	£855	Three miles and six furlongs
1 Skyreholme (N. Crump)	8-10-13	A.P. Thompson
2 Fighting Line (K. Cundell)	12-9-9	C. Smithers
3 Brown Hall (T.H. Yates)	11-10-12	T. Molony

Winning owner Mr C.F. Booth

16 ran.   Distances: a head, 15l, 20l.   SP 7/2 fav., 10/1, 5/1.   Going good.

Skyreholme, chestnut gelding by Hastings-Upney Lane

1952

Despite incessant rain the biggest Chepstow crowd in years saw ex-selling plater Dinton Lass give Alf Mullins his second Welsh Grand National winner. King Stephen and Goodbye Dolly made the early running and after Lady Hague's Kelek had refused at the first Klaxton and Castleknock both fell on the first circuit.

Goodbye Dolly was still in front when she sped past the stands, but she struck her hind legs in the water jump and blundered away her chances. Approaching the last only three lengths or so separated the first six who were, in order of running, Dinton Lass, King Stephen, Head Crest, Ordnance, Glen Fire and Frere Jean. However, Dinton Lass ran on in game style and at the winning post had two lengths in hand over Head Crest with Ordnance a further five lengths away in third place. Winning owner Ernest Excell recalled, 'It rained all day and the going was very heavy which suited Dinton Lass. She was very small just half-an-inch above 15 hands high. But with her low weight the conditions were in her favour.' Mr Excell added, 'But she never won another race afterwards and although she dropped three foals when put to stud none of them managed to win a race.'

Mr Ernest Excell's Dinton Lass.

Dinton Lass (no. 13) gives Alf Mullins his second Welsh Grand National success in 1952.

Between 1946-53 Dinton Lass won ten races and five of these were at Chepstow Racecourse the scene of her greatest success. A bargain buy at 100 guineas she was trained by John Roberts the son of Welsh-born trainer Ben Roberts at Cheltenham who two years later went on to train the Cheltenham Gold Cup winner Four Ten.

Alf Mullins, who had turned professional just before the start of the Second World War, was to ride around two hundred winners over the sticks. He died in August 1976 at the comparatively young age of sixty-three.

Monday 14 April	£855		Three miles and six furlongs
1 Dinton Lass (J. Roberts)	10-10-0	Alf Mullins	
2 Head Crest (G. Wilson)	6-10-2	S. Barnes	
3 Ordnance (T.F. Rimell)	6-10-12	M Scudamore	

Winning owner Mr Ernest Excell
16 ran. Distances: 2l, 5l, short head. SP 10/1, 10/1, 8/1.
Fav. Glen Fire 7/2 (5th). Going heavy.
Dinton Lass, bay mare by Ximeenes-Spancil Hill

1953

With perfect spring weather and a big crowd, fourteen of the seventy-seven entries faced the starter in 1953. Mr Henry William Dufosee's homebred Stalbridge Rock, which was trained by him at Stalbridge Park in Dorset, was ridden to success by twenty-two-year-old amateur rider Bob McCreery the son of General Sir Richard McCreery, the owner and a director of Wincanton Racecourse who had won the Military Gold Cup on Dash O'White in 1923.

Well placed throughout the race, Stalbridge Rock, who stood around 15.3 hands high, moved up down the back straight to take the lead approaching the last fence to win by a neck from Tommy Cullen's mount Pactol. Mr McCreery had this to say to Pat Lucas, 'I originally rode Stalbridge Rock at Liverpool in 1951 when twelve horses fell at the first fence. I was working at a University in America, but I stayed on to ride Stalbridge Rock in the Welsh National because we thought he had a good chance in it, which proved to be true. As I remember it, he was well placed all the way until I took closer order down the back side and hit the front just before the last fence. In the Liverpool race he over-jumped at the first and turned completely over, but in the Welsh National he ran well throughout.'

McCreery, who had ridden his first winner on Alacrity at Wolverhampton in 1949, tied for the amateur riders' championship in 1955/56 with Mr A. Moralee with 13 winners apiece. But in the 1956/57 season he won the title outright with 23 winners. On a horse called Gold Wire he won 21 races including the Prix St Saveur at Auteuil. He rode winners in the USA, Sweden, Spain and France, and when he hung up his riding boots he turned to breeding horses and he bred the 2000 Guineas winner High Top. Stalbridge Rock, who was originally trained by Ivor Anthony, won seven steeplechases and five hurdle races from 66 starts in a career that spanned ten seasons.

Tuesday 7 April	£855	Three miles and six furlongs
1 Stalbridge Rock (H. Dufosee)	10-11-3	Mr Robert McCreery
2 Pactol (W. McMullen)	7-10-3	T. Cullen
3 Cordon Rouge (K. Cundell)	10-11-0	Mr A. Corbett

Winning owner Mr W.H. Dufosee
15 ran.   Distances: neck, 6l, 2l.   SP 6/1, 10/1, 7/2 fav.   Going soft.
Stalbridge Rock, bay gelding by Blunderbuss-Rock Honey

1954

Thirty-five-year-old former flat jockey John Hunter, who had won his first race on the flat in Jersey some seventeen years earlier, rode around 350 winners. But his success in this year's Welsh Grand National on Blow Horn, on his own admission, was the highlight of his race-riding career. Unconquered, ridden by Victor Speck, after leading the field of seventeen runners for almost two thirds of the race faded out leaving Gay Donald in the lead from Filaki. The favourite Bar Point unseated his rider at the fence before the water jump. Blow Horn came into prominence six fences from home and began his challenge a couple of furlongs from the finish which he maintained all the way to the line to beat Filaki by one-and-a-half lengths. Gay Donald was third and Halloween fourth. Mount St Michael, who had been well placed for three miles, was lying third when he fell in the closing stages.

Recalling the race, John Hunter said, 'Although only small Blow Horn was a genuine, dead honest sort. We were in the middle division throughout the early part of the race, but made up ground steadily and jumped to the front at the last.' Blow Horn was trained by Tommy Jarvis a farmer from Knightsbridge in Devon and Hunter won nine races on him. Blow Horn's owner, Herbert Roger Morgan, aged thirty-six, a Devonshire farmer, used to ride in point-to-points and as a permit holder himself won the Halloween Chase at Newbury with Sacrilege. He was first

Blow Horn (no. 10) jumps into the lead in the 1954 Welsh Grand National.

THIRD RACE.—Three Miles and Six Furlongs.   Yellow Armlet.

3.15—WELSH GRAND NATIONAL (handicap steeple chase)
of 1250 sov.; second to receive 250 sov. and the third 125 sov. out of the plate; for five yrs old and upwards; the highest handicap weight to be not more than 12st 7lb; the winner, after the publication of the weights (April 1st, at noon), of a steeple chase of three miles or over to carry 5lb, of two such steeple chases, or of any steeple chase value 400 sov., 9lb extra, but horses originally handicapped at 12st or over to be exempt from penalties; entrance 10 sov., and 10 sov. extra if forfeit be not declared to Messrs Weatherby and Sons, or to Messrs Pratt and Co., by April 6th; three miles, six furlongs (59 entries, forfeit declared for 37).—Closed February 2nd, 1954.

		Age	st	lb		Trainer
1	HALLOWEEN.................... (Contessa di Sant Elia) Br g Court Nez—My Blue Heaven	a	12	0	Cerise, white hoop and cap	W. Wightman
2	FREEBOOTER (Mrs L. Brotherton) B g Steel-point—Proud Fury	a	11	10	Blue and silver (halved), blue sleeves, scarlet cap	R. Renton
3	GAY DONALD (Mr G. A. Burt) ... B g Gaylight—Pas de Quatre	a	11	6	Blue, yellow sash, red hooped sleeves, qtd cap	J. Ford
4	WHISPERING STEEL.................... (Mr F. H. Curnick) B g Steel-point—Boltown	a	10	11	Blue, white hoop and arm-lets, white cap, blue spots	A. Kilpatrick
5	WILLOWHILL (Mrs F. Walwyn)... Br g Kings Approach—Silly Beck	a	10	10	Champagne, claret hoop, striped cap	F. Walwyn
6	KLAXTON (Major W. D. Gibson)... B g Mr Toots—Orchardstown Lass	a	10	10	Black, red, white and blue sash and cap	R. Turnell
7	GLENBEIGH (Miss Dorothy Paget) B g Cameron—Golden Wave	a	10	9	Blue, yellow hoop, yellow cap, blue hoop	F. Walwyn
8	PACTOL (Mrs J. E. Westray) ...... Br g Pactolus—Tolgissa	a	10	2	Gold, black spots, green cap	W. McMullen
9	HEAD CREST (Mr G. H. Dowty) Br or br m Headway—Cresserelle (in. 9lb ex.)	a	10	2	Scarlet, green sleeves, halved cap	Gerald Wilson
10	BLOW HORN (Mrs S. M. Morgan).. Br g J'Accours—Blow Soft	a	10	1	Maroon and old gold (quartered)	T. Jarvis
11	FILAKI (Mr H. Gibbon).............. B h Mieuxcé—Carissa	a	10	1	Yellow, black V and cap	H. Price
12	CORDON ROUGE (Mr W. J. Oliver)	a	10	1		F. Bushell
13	OUTLAW (Mr ...).................... (Col. M. Gordon Watson) Ch g Within-the-Law—Greenridge	a	10	1	Black, light blue cross-belts and sleeves	P. Payne-Gallwey
14	JO HUKUM (Miss J. A. Millar)...... B h Ujiji—Science	a	9	13	Sky blue black sleeves and collar, blue cuffs	A. Piper
15	CAFE CREME (Mrs F. B. Watkins) Ch g Sir Nigel, or Cappielo—Creme Chocolate	a	9	12	Crimson, yellow sleeves, purple cap	P. Payne-Gallwey
16	MONT ST MICHEL (Mrs F. Clarke) Br g Mieuxcé—Hillhampton	a	9	10	Mauve, white star, black sleeves and cap	J. Clarke
17	GAY FOX (Miss R. Cates)............ Br g Fearless Fox—Wayward Spirit	a	9	8	Amber, old rose cross-belts	C. Cooper
18	UNCONQUERED (Lord Bicester).... Br g Cameron—Silver Cat	a	9	7	Black, gold sleeves, red cap	G. Beeby
19	NOBLE METAL (Mrs A. Warman) Br g Young Lover—Vanadium	6	9	7	Royal blue, yellow halved sleeves and peak of cap	J. Hamey
20	RED MEAD (Mr F. S. Jordison) ... B or br g Red Shaft—Galomead	a	9	7	Royal blue, scarlet sash and cap	T. F. Rimell
21	BAR POINT (Col. Stanley Bell) ... B h Steel-point—Hopeful Lady	a	9	7	Blue, white cross-belts, pink and blue quartered cap	R. Renton
22	MARTINIQUE (Mr A. Greenberg) B g Mieuxcé—Carouse	a	9	7	White, green sleeves and sash, quartered cap	G. R. Owen

Chepstow racecard, 1954.

attracted to Blow Horn when it beat his own horse Cracker at Newton Abbot and bought him for just 160 guineas. Blow Horn used to run in bumpers in Ireland and when he was first brought to England he was trained by Ken Cundell, but later moved to Fred Rimell's yard. It is worth recalling that the following year, 1955, Gay Donald won the Cheltenham Gold Cup beating Halloween by ten lengths. The latter, a dual winner of the King George VI Chase, was placed in the Gold Cup four times but never managed to win it.

Tuesday 20 April	£855		Three miles and six furlongs

1	Blow Horn (T. Jarvis)	10-10-6	John Hunter
2	Filaki (H.R. Price)	9-10-3	Mr J.S. Evans
3	Gay Donald (J. Ford)	8-11-6	A. Grantham

Winning owner Mrs S.M. Morgan

17 ran.   Distances: 1½l, short head, 2l.   SP 100/8, 20/1, 6/1.

Fav. Bar Point 5/1 unseated rider.

Blow Horn, brown gelding by J'Accours-Blow Soft

1955

Monaleen, a ten-year-old bay gelding who stood 16.3h.h., and who had been bought after a win at Galway in Ireland by Mr Herbert Thomson Smith, of Braintree in Essex, was the 20/1 shock winner of this year's race. The prolific winner Crudwell, joint favourite with Sundew, was well placed at halfway but was hampered when Barn Close fell at the sixteenth fence and eventually finished tenth. Monaleen, who had failed to win in his previous 18 starts, was in sixth place approaching the last fence but he finished so strongly under Paddy Fitzgerald that he won by half-a-length from Sundew partnered by the great Fred Winter. Clearing, seventh in the Aintree National, finished third and Valiant Spark was fourth. Mr Thomson Smith's daughter, Mrs Janet Wooton, said, 'I was only twelve at the time but I remember that it was an exciting race. Monaleen finished so fast after the last fence it looked as though it was a flat race. He was one of the sweetest horses my father trained, a family pet really, but he tragically broke a bone in his leg a few years later at Fontwell.'

Monaleen, who was by the Lincolnshire Handicap winner Over Coat, nearly didn't run in the race. 'It was touch and go as the day before he appeared slightly lame, but when we walked him the next morning he was sound', added Mrs Wooton who said all that she could remember about Monaleen's jockey was that, 'He spoke in a real broad Irish accent and was over the moon when he won.'

For thirty-six-year-old Patrick Fitzgerald, who had notched-up his first winner at Windsor in 1948 at the tender age of sixteen, Monaleen's win was to prove the high

Paddy Fitzgerald who won the 1955 race on Monaleen.

Mr H.T. Smith's 1955 Welsh Grand National winner Monaleen. The young girl on the left is Mr and Mrs Smith's daughter, Janet (now Mrs Janet Wooton).

point of his race riding career. Paddy, who went to the same school in Ireland as the immortal trainer Vincent O'Brien, reminisced, 'I jogged around Chepstow Racecourse at midnight before the race so that I could make the weight. Monaleen was a fine horse who not only beat Sundew, a Grand National winner, but on another occasion also beat a Gold Cup winner in Gay Donald. He was a lovely ride but only had the one run and I jumped the last slightly behind Fred Winter.'

As for the runner-up Sundew, two years later this big chestnut gelding went on to win the 1957 Aintree National with Fred Winter in the saddle. Sadly, later that same year, he broke a shoulder at Haydock and had to be put down. He was buried on the racecourse.

Tuesday 12 April	£855	Three miles and six furlongs
1 Monaleen (T. Smith)	10-9-7	Paddy Fitzgerald
2 Sundew (J. McClintock)	9-11-3	F. Winter
3 Clearing (W. Stephenson)	8-9-13	R. Hamey

Winning owner Mr H.T. Smith

17 ran.   Distances: 1l, ½l, same.   SP 20/1, 3/1 jt. fav., 100/8.

Other joint fav. Crudwell (10th).

Monaleen, bay gelding by Over Coat-Marcia

1956

For the first time in its history the Welsh Grand National was broadcast to racegoers on the track by former England and Glamorgan County cricketer Johnny Clay who was assisted by Mrs C.C. Williams, later to become a steward at the course.

Dick Francis, robbed of a Grand National win earlier on Devon Loch who had mysteriously collapsed just fifty yards or so from the winning post, gained some sort of compensation when landing his second Welsh Grand National on Crudwell. The plucky Pembrokeshire-born Welshman rode a patient race and did not send the ten-year-old to the front until approaching three fences from the finish. The Welsh-trained Billy Budd cut out the early pace while the mare Tiberetta was in close attendance throughout most of the race.

However, in a great dash to the winning post, Crudwell snatched the verdict by a head from Billy Budd with Tiberetta a further two lengths away third and Four Ten the 1954 Cheltenham Gold Cup hero fourth. Tiberetta was to prove she was more suited to the Aintree National . In the 1957 race she was third, second in 1958 and fourth in 1959. Frank Cundell, who trained Crudwell, had good cause to celebrate that day as Crudwell was the third leg of a treble with him having won the first two races with Torrent IV and John's Company respectively.

A former successful amateur rider and veterinary surgeon Frank Cundell died in 1983 at the age of seventy-three after being in ill health for some months. Dick Francis, in his autobiography *The Sport of Queens* (Michael Joseph 1957) wrote, 'Devon Loch and the Grand National were still in my mind when Crudwell and I set off ten days later for our second try at the Welsh National. As he had grown older his finishing speed had not deserted him, but he could no longer risk lying too far back during the early stages of the race, so I planned to take him gradually to the front and not leave him too much to do at the end. All went well until the third last fence, where Crudwell made a slight mistake. He jumped the next fence very cautiously, and two horses, both carrying very light weights, which had been level with us, went on in front. As we followed them over the last fence I thought there was little hope of catching them again, but Crudwell fought on with his old flying speed and won the race in the last few strides.'

The popular Crudwell, who was bred in Crudwell, Wiltshire, by Mrs E.E. Large, was Britain's most prolific winner of the twentieth century. During a long and esteemed racing career he won seven Flat races, four hurdle events and thirty-nine chases out of a total of 108 races and was placed on a further 32 other occasions.

Jack Fawxus, who rode four
Welsh Grand National winners.

Tuesday 3 April	**£855**	**Three miles and six furlongs**
1 Crudwell (F. Cundell)	10-11-6	Dick Francis
2 Billy Budd (E.C. Morel)	6-9-8	H. Lewis
3 Tiberetta (E. Courage)	8-9-12	A. Oughton

Winning owner Mrs D.M. Cooper

16 ran.   Distances: head, 2l, 1l.   SP 100/9, 33/1, 100/7.

Fav. Must 11/4 (6th)   Going firm.

Crudwell, bay gelding by Noble Star-Alexandrina

The Master of Kinnersley, the late great trainer Fred Rimell, saddled the first of his four Welsh Grand National winners when Charlie Nixon's Creeola II out-jumped several Aintree starters to win this year's race. Creeola II, who was Rimell's fortieth winner of the season, disputed the lead more or less from the start with Billy Budd. The 1954 Cheltenham Gold Cup winner Four Ten and the gallant Aintree specialist Tiberetta, who had earlier finished third in the Aintree National , both strongly challenged in the closing stages but were comfortably held by the ex-Irish horse whom Mr Nixon had bought four years previously for £200 from Captain C. Harty who had won two hunter chases and eight point-to-points with him including the 1955 Lady Dudley Cup.

Farmer's son Michael Scudamore, who had won this year's Cheltenham Gold Cup on Linwell, was the winning jockey and he said, 'I had a marvellous ride. Creeola II hung a little bit, but he jumped brilliantly throughout.' Two years later Scudamore, who had ridden his first winner at Chepstow when a young lad of seventeen, won the Aintree National on Oxo. The 1956/57 season was his best winner-wise as he rode 58 winners to finish runner-up in the jockey's championship.

Tuesday 23 April	£855		Three miles and six furlongs
1 Creeola II (T.F. Rimell)	9-10-5		Michael Scudamore
2 Four Ten (A. Kilpatrick)	11-11-8		R. Morrow
3 Tiberetta (E. Courage)	9-9-12		A. Oughton

Winning owner Mr Charlie Nixon

11 ran.   Distances: 2l, 4l, 1l.   SP 3/1 fav., 10/1, 10/1.   Going firm.

Creeola II, chestnut gelding by King's Approach-Old Friend

1958

Only seven of the fourteen starters in this year's race completed the course. The field got away to a good start with Briggate leading over the first fence. At the eighth fence, Stan Mellor's mount Honourless jumped ahead of Briggate with Tiger William and Devil's Luck not far behind. Devil's Luck's hind legs went into the water jump and this put paid to any chances he might have had. The thirteenth fence proved unlucky for Tiger William as he came down while Honourless was a casualty at the sixteenth.

Oscar Wilde, who had been last all the way on the first circuit, after gradually moving up through the field under Brian Lawrence's strong riding, had joined the new leader Crudwell, ridden this time by Fred Winter, at the second last and although making a complete hash of it went on to win an exciting race by three parts of a length.

The 1956 winner Crudwell with 12st 1lb on his back was giving more than two stone away to Oscar Wilde and perhaps if Fred Winter had been harder on the horse he might have won. Nevertheless, full credit must go to Oscar Wilde's rider Brian Lawrence who was chalking-up only the second win of his riding career.

Brian Lawrence who rode the 1958 winner Oscar Wilde.

Oscar Wilde jumps the last fence ahead of Crudwell to win the 1958 race.
(Photograph courtesy of B. Lawrence)

Oscar Wilde, who went on to win the Walton Green Handicap at Sandown Park in 1958 and 1959, was owned by Southampton solicitor Mr Thomas T. Jasper who said at the time, 'This is the first horse I have owned. I leased him from Mr Delahooke a Buckingham farmer last November and this is the first time he has won in three years.'

A 20/1 outsider, Oscar Wilde was something of an awkward jumper in his early days, and was trained by W.G.R. Wightman who had been training horses since 1937.

Tuesday 8 April	£855		Three miles and six furlongs
1 Oscar Wilde (W. Wightman)	8-9-13		Brian Lawrence
2 Crudwell (F. Cundell)	12-12-1		F. Winter
3 Mr Gay (P. Thrale)	11-11-3		D. Ancil

Winning owner Mr Thomas T. Jasper
14 ran.   Distances: ¾l. 6l. 20l.   SP 20/1, 8/1, 5/2 fav.   Going good.
Oscar Wilde, bay gelding by Epigram-Queenington

1959

For Mrs G.R. 'Posy' Lewis, a director of Chepstow Racecourse, it was a case of third time lucky when she saw her eight-year-old Limonali run out an easy winner of the 1959 race. For in past years her Billy Budd and Waving Star had been narrowly beaten in the race she wanted so much to win. An 100/8 outsider, Limonali finished strongly to beat the previous year's winner Oscar Wilde by six lengths. Arthur Freeman on Mac Joy finished third and Prune was fourth. In fifth place came Master Copper ridden by his owner/trainer Colin Davies, who had won the classic Lady Dudley Cup point-to-point race on him in 1958. The only horse to fall was the favourite The Bell.

David Nicholson on Limonali on their way to winning their first Welsh Grand National in 1959.

Ridden by David Nicholson, who was putting up 2lb overweight, Limonali who was always prominent throughout took up the running after the seventeenth fence to score a popular win for Wales. Described by David Nicholson as a rough coated little rabbit, Limonali had been bought by Mrs Lewis from his Irish breeder Dr Stokes some eighteen months earlier. 'He was not too good in himself so I gave him the old Irish treatment of turning him out in the paddock letting him roll in the mud and it did the trick', recalled Mrs Lewis.

At six feet one inch there weren't many taller National Hunt jockeys than David Nicholson. He had ridden his first winner at Chepstow four years earlier when just sixteen and his win in this year's Welsh Grand National was his biggest at the time. The son of the famed 'Frenchie' Nicholson, David was known as 'The Duke' because of his handsome looks and smart appearance. Taffy Jenkins from Maesteg, who rode the runner-up, partnered more than 100 winners between 1951 and 1962, but unfortunately he had as many falls as he had winners and his riding career came to an end after a crashing fall at Sandown in 1963 which left him in a very bad way. He started training sometime afterwards and it was something of a coincidence that the track which ended his riding career got him off to a start as a trainer when Voleur won there in 1966.

Tuesday 31 March	£1,030		Three miles and six furlongs
1 Limonali (E.C. Morel)	8-10-2		David Nicholson
2 Oscar Wilde (W. Wightman)	9-10-9		R.E. Jenkins
3 Mac Joy (K. Bailey)	7-10-11		A. Freeman

Winning owner Mrs G.R. Lewis

10 ran.   Distances: 6l. 15l. 8l.   SP 100/8, 7/2, 100/8.   Fav. The Bell 5/2 (fell).

Going very holding.

Limonali, bay gelding by Hyder-Limonetta

1960

The going was on the good side for the 1960 Welsh Grand National and ten of the fourteen starters completed the course. David Nicholson, later to become a leading trainer, had the ride on former Welsh point-to-pointer Clover Bud owned and trained by Tenby farmer Gordon Llewellin. Always in a handy position throughout the race, Clover Bud scored an easy fifteen-lengths win from Skatealong with The Bell, a faller the previous year, a further three lengths away third. Clover Bud, a game bay mare, was timed at 7 minutes 36.5 seconds, which was very fast indeed. On dismounting, Nicholson, aged twenty-one, said, 'I went to the front approaching the sixteenth and from that moment I always felt confident that I would win.'

Clover Bud, who had started the 1959 point-to-point season as a maiden, had been hunted with the South Pembrokeshire pack. She had finished unplaced in

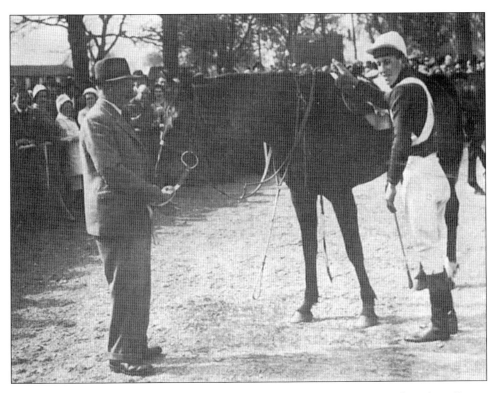

Clover Bud, the 1960 Welsh Grand National winner, with owner Gordon Llewellin and winning jockey David Nicholson.

her first race, but went on to win her remaining six races that season. It was at the Carmarthenshire, at St Clears, that she lost her maiden tag when beating Chavara a horse who figures in our story later. A week later at the South Pembrokeshire, at Lydstep, she won from Cefn Fancy. Graduating to open class, she accounted for Carberry Belle at the Llandilo Farmers and then beat two prolific winners – Stony Bridge and Cariff Princess – at the Llangeinor.

After a brilliant win in the Lady Dudley Cup at the Worcestershire Hunt, Clover Bud, who was ridden in all these races by Mr Llewellin's son Derrick, won a hunter' chase at Hereford. She was tough as old boots and won six more races under National Hunt rules and raced until she was fifteen. She covered more than 150 miles of National Hunt fences and only on one occasion – when falling at the first fence in the Aintree National – did she fall. An out-and-out stayer she won the Fred Withington Chase at Cheltenham over three miles and seven furlongs and a four miler at Birmingham. She was in training for a short spell with Fred Rimell, but soon returned to her owner.

Later she initiated her stud career with two sets of dead twins, but was to prove most successful at stud in later years. Clover Bud died at the ripe old age of twenty-seven and produced Captain Clover and champion point-to-point winner National Clover who was the dam of that good horse Go Ballistic.

Tuesday 19 April	**£1,030**		**Three miles and six furlongs**
1 Clover Bud (G. Llewellin)	10-10-10	David Nicholson
2 Skatelong (H. Thomson-Jones)	12-9-12	R. Harrison
3 The Bell (T.H. Yates)	9-12-0	B. Lawrence

Winning owner Mr Gordon Llewellin

14 ran.   15l. 3l. 4l.   SP: 7/1, 100/7, 13/2   Fav. Isle of Skye 9/2 (fell).

Going good.

Clover Bud, brown mare by Phebus-The Hayseed

1961

David Nicholson made it three wins in a row when landing the 1961 race on little Limonali. Having been successful the previous year on Clover Bud and the year before that on Limonali he had the choice of riding either and, as luck would have it, he picked the right one. Limonali in winning the race for the second time gave a brilliant display of jumping in blinding rain and in doing so beat two other Welsh horses Chavara and Clover Bud.

According to the racecard, Limonali was trained by Mrs Lewis's son Ifor and when he had won in 1959 her brother Clem Morel was down as the trainer. But almost everyone knew that the horse was trained by his owner. Women in those days were not allowed to train. Mrs Posy Lewis, who received a great ovation in the unsaddling enclosure, recalled, 'We had prayed for rain and it came just in time. Limonali was kicked by another jockey's stirrup in the Hennessy two years before and he literally had a chip on his shoulder which moved about beneath his skin until it eventually attached itself to the shoulder bone again.'

In the race itself, Stan Mellor jumped Chavara to the front six fences from home, but immediately David Nicholson had Limonali at his girths. From then on the race developed into a great dual with Limonali who never put a foot wrong throughout the stamina-sapping journey jumping fractionally ahead at each of the remaining fences. A mistake by Chavara at the third last did not improve Mellor's chances of overtaking Limonali who produced a good turn of speed to pass the winning post five lengths clear. Clover Bud, this time ridden by David Mould, ran on gamely to finish a further two lengths back in third spot with Knockanacunna, ridden by Michael Scudamore, finishing in fourth and last place.

Tuesday 4 April	£1,030		Three miles and six furlongs
1 Limonali (I. Lewis)	10-11-12	David Nicholson	
2 Chavara (G.R. Owen)	8-11-13	S. Mellor	
3 Clover Bud (G. Llewellin)	11-11-7	D. Mould	

Winning owner Mrs Posy Lewis

9 ran.　　Distances 5l. 2l. 10l.　　SP 7/4 fav., 3/1, 8/1.　　Going very soft.

Limonali, bay gelding by Hyder Ali-Limonette

1962

Forty Secrets, owned by Warwickshire solicitor Alan David Clark, was successful in this year's race. The eight-year-old son of Fortina won unchallenged by fifteen lengths after making all the running. The runner-up Strat Royal made some headway in the closing stages, but never looked like catching Forty Secrets and only held on to second place by half-a-length from Motel who was to win the race the following year. Sir William Pigott-Brown on the top-weighted Superfine, who started favourite, finished fourth.

Forty Secret's sire, Fortina, is the only entire to have won the Cheltenham Gold Cup. He sired many winners including the winners of two Cheltenham Gold Cups in Fort Leney (1968) and Glencaraig Lady (1972). Forty Secrets was ridden by twenty-one-year-old Josh Gifford, a former flat race jockey who this season won the first of his four champion jockey titles. Gifford, who was to ride 642 winners between 1959 and 1970 when he took out a trainers' licence, has saddled many big race winners including the 1981 Grand National hero Aldaniti. Recalling the race he said, 'I don't think I had any nasty moments in the race, except that I got a bit close to the second last. But he was a very fast jumping horse – didn't get as high as he might have done – but always quick and athletic. He stayed all day, and loved the soft.'

One of the amateur riders who finished among the also-rans on his own horse Claymore was Mr Colin Davies a former car racing driver who was later to become famous as the trainer of triple Champion Hurdler Persian War. He was to fulfil a personal ambition by completing the Aintree Grand National course on Claymore in 1964. Forty Secrets was trained by Cheltenham's Earl Jones whom, as we shall see, was to win the race again.

Tuesday 24 April	£855	Three miles and six furlongs

1	Forty Secrets (Earl Jones)	8-10-11	Josh Gifford
2	Strat Royal (S. Cuff)	8-11-5	J. Curran
3	Motel (W. Lowe)	8-11-0	Mr G. Small

Winning owner Mr Alan David Clark

15 ran.   Distances: 15l. 1/2l. 5l.   SP 6/1, 100/8, 9/1   Superfine 3/1 fav. (4th).

Going good with soft patches.

Forty Secrets, bay gelding by Fortina-Secret

1963

Former dual Welsh Grand National winner Limonali made most of the early running in this year's race but coming into the straight it was Jungle Beach who led from Motel with the tiring Limonali back in third spot. Approaching the last, Jungle Beach was still ahead of Motel but he checked on landing allowing Motel to gain a lead of one-and-a-half lengths which he maintained all the way to the winning post. Wartown, ridden by Eddie Harty, finished third ahead of Limonali.

Motel was a lucky chance ride for thirty-one-year-old Paddy Cowley as Fred Winter, who was down to ride the horse, injured his ribs when riding in the first race and could not take the ride. Paddy's son Simon Cowley recalled, 'Paddy got the ride on Motel as Fred was injured in a fall after being brought down by my father! Dad took Fred home that night since he was in no state to drive.' But despite his misfortune Fred could see the funny side of it and arriving home he told him, 'You turn me over at the ditch, ride my horse to victory in the big race and now you sit here drinking my whisky!'

The race was marred by the death of the favourite Shavings who came down at a fence entering the straight on the second circuit. The heavily-backed Shavings never showed throughout and was believed to have broken a blood vessel and was already dead when the veterinary surgeon got to him.

Motel, who only raced for two seasons, was trained by fifty-nine-year-old permit holder Mr William King Lowe at Fox Farm, in Stow-on-the-Wold, Gloucestershire, the venue for many years of the Heythrop Hunt Point-To-Point. Paddy Cowley came over from Ireland to ride chiefly for Phil Doherty and Hugh Summer and had ridden his first winner in Ireland fourteen years earlier.

Tuesday 16 April	£855		Three miles and six furlongs
1 Motel (W.K. Lowe)	9-10-6		Paddy Cowley
2 Jungle Beach (T.F. Rimell)	6-10-11		T. Biddlecombe
3 Wartown (R.C. Price)	12-10-0		E.P. Harty

Winning owner Mr W.K. Lowe

15 Ran.   Distances: 1½l, 15l.   SP 7/1, 7/1, 33/1.   Fav. Shavings 5/2 (fell).

Going soft.

Motel, bay gelding by Mush-Ponderosa

1964

Bishop Aukland trainer Arthur Stephenson, who had won the 1961 Scottish Grand National with Kinmont Willie, wasn't at Chepstow to see his first runner at the track land the 1964 Welsh Grand National with increased prize-money a record £1,738 to the winner. His eight-year-old mare Rainbow Battle, having only her seventh race over fences, dictated the early pace on the first circuit with Limonali. However, at the fifteenth fence, Limonali's hind legs went into the water jump virtually putting him out of the race.

On Account then took up the running and was still going great guns when falling five fences from home leaving Rainbow Battle in the lead. Moyrath, ridden by Harry Beasley, challenged strongly but Rainbow Battle, under Paddy Broderick's strong driving, and despite pecking at the last, repelled the challenge to win by two lengths. The game little Limonali was a similar distance away in third with Jacalocher back in fourth place.

Arthur Stephenson, who had had a four-timer the previous day at his favourite track Wetherby, had bought Rainbow Battle only six months previously and the following year she was to finish fourth at Aintree. She was retired to stud shortly afterwards and was the dam of Gylippus who later figures in our story in somewhat dramatic circumstances. Paddy Broderick, who was immensely popular with his fellow jockeys, said, 'As soon as I saw On Account fall on entering the straight I knew I would win so well was the mare running. I realised that Moyrath was making up ground steadily approaching the final fence but Rainbow Battle, game mare that she is, held off the challenge.'

Arthur Stephenson, who in the 1969/70 season was to become the first National Hunt trainer to saddle 100 winners – 114 to be exact and he repeated the feat in six of the next seven seasons – trained many big race winners including the 1987 Cheltenham Gold Cup winner The Thinker. He wasn't at Cheltenham that day either being found much closer to home at Hexham watching his appropriately named Succeeded win a lowly three-mile handicap 'chase. Never one to hog the limelight, he died in South Cleveland Hospital, Middlesborough, after a long illness in December 1992. During his lifetime, he trained 2,645 winners over the jumps and 344 winners on the flat which at the time was surely some sort of record.

OFFICIAL RACE CARD　　　**PRICE ONE SHILLING**

CHEPSTOW
EASTER MEETING

UNDER NATIONAL HUNT RULES AND THE CHEPSTOW RACE CLUB

Second Day - Tuesday, April 20th, 1954

PATRON.

Captain A. W. WINGATE.

STEWARDS.

H. A. CLIVE, Esq., M.C.　　　Lt.-Colonel G. MORGAN-JONES.
Lt.-Colonel H. M. LLEWELLYN, C.B.E.　　Major R. STIRLING-STUART.

OFFICIALS.

Stewards' Secretary - Rear-Admiral H. B. JACOMB.
Handicapper - Mr. J. H. MEREDITH.　*Starter* - Capt. G. R. CHANDOS-POLE.
Judge - Mr. C. G. SEYMOUR.　*Clerk of the Scales* - Mr. J. R. H. WARREN.
Veterinary Surgeons - Mr. T. T. McNAUGHT, M.R.C.V.S., and Mr. G. TREANOR, M.R.C.V.S.

Surgeons in Attendance

Dr. MAURICE HORAN, F.R.C.S.　　Dr. H. JOSTE-SMITH, M.C., M.B., B.S.
Auctioneer - Mr. F. H. TRANTER.
Stakeholders - Messrs. WEATHERBY AND SONS.
Clerk of the Course - Sir KENNETH GIBSON, 17, Welsh Street, Chepstow.
Club Secretary and Manager - Mr. R. L. CLAY, 17, Welsh Street, Chepstow.
Secretary to the Company - Mr. G. L. B. FRANCIS, 17, Welsh Street, Chepstow.

Published by Authority of the Clerk of the Course and printed by
WEATHERBY & SONS, Campden Hill Road, London, W.8.

Chepstow Racecard, Welsh Grand National day, 20 April 1954.

Tuesday 31 March	£1,738	Three miles and six furlongs

1	Rainbow Battle (W.A. Stephenson)	8-10-0	Paddy Broderick
2	Moyrath (A. Thomas)	11-10-5	H. Beasley
3	Limonali (C. Carpenter)	13-10-7	D. Nicholson

Winning owner Mr W.A. Stephenson

11 ran.　Distances: 2l, 2l, 2l.　SP 3/1 fav., 100/8, 5/1.　Going soft.

Rainbow Battle, bay mare by Raincheck-Duel in the Sun

1965

One horse who created a big impression in Welsh point-to-points during the 1964 season was Glanville Jones's Norther who had been qualified with the Pentyrch Hunt. On two occasions Norther, who loved munching those mints with a hole in the middle, had beaten Snowdra Queen the mare brought out of Wales by Mrs Jackie Brutton and who was to win, among other races, the United Hunts Challenge Cup at Cheltenham.

Led over the last by Quintina, who was trying to land a notable double for trainer Fred Winter who had saddled Jay Trump to win the Aintree National , Norther stayed on gallantly to beat Fred Winter's charge by a length with Dark Venetian pipping Limonali for third place. Norther was Terry Biddlecombe's 99th winner of the season. Norther, who was landing his fifth win of the season, was trained by Denzil Jenkins of Cowbridge in the Vale of Glamorgan.

During the Second World War, Sqdn Ldr Jenkins, DFC, had commanded a squadron of fighter pilots and had 192 flying operations to his credit. He declared, 'He was bred well enough to win anything being by Precipitation and Terry was very confident that day.' Mr Jones though was surprised as he thought his horse had been given too much weight. Usually, Norther was ridden by Ken White but he had been claimed to ride Pallas Main who finished fifth. Sadly, the Grand National third Mr Jones had a fatal fall at the water jump and his rider Chris Collins was not only badly shaken but had a nasty leg gash. Terry Biddlecombe's brother, Tony, also had good reason to remember this particular Chepstow meeting. He rode a hat-trick!

The following year, Norther finished seventh in the Aintree National and was second in the Scottish Grand National. A fine jumper he was to return to point-to-pointing and had only one fall since 1966 when at the age of fifteen he came down at the first fence at the South Pembrokeshire. He sadly somehow broke his jaw when grazing in his field and had to be put down.

Tuesday 20 April	£1,755		Three miles and six furlongs
1 Norther (D. Jenkins)	8-11-0		Terry Biddlecombe
2 Quintina (F. Winter)	9-10-1		E.P. Harty
3 Dark Venetian (D. Barons)	10-10-5		J. Renfree

Winning owner Mr Glanville Jones

11 ran.   Distances: 1l, 6l, head.   SP 9/2, 2/1 fav., 8/1.   Going good.

Norther, bay gelding by Precipitation-Serenoa

1966

Twenty-two-year-old West countryman Tim Norman, who had been successful on 50/1 chance Anglo in this year's Aintree National, won this year's race on Madame Borel de Bitche's Kilburn.

Kilburn, who was over seventeen hands high, and a very game and bold jumper, was always in the leading group, and revelling in the heavy ground he out-jumped his ten rivals to score by three lengths from the locally-trained horse Cotswold after taking over the lead five fences from home. Cotswold, under Steve 'Buster' Rooney, and trained by Chepstow's Colin Davies, staged a strong challenge from the last fence but Kilburn, who was winning for the fourth time this season, always had that little bit extra. The favourite Jomsviking, partnered by Jeff King, was a further five lengths away in third place with Pearlita back in fourth.

Trained in East Kent by Chris Nesfield, Kilburn had been bought in Ireland four years earlier in the hope that he would make a good show-jumper! The only mistake he made during the race was when he met the open ditch on the far side of the course all wrong, but cleverly, or it could have been luckily, kept his feet. It was later discovered that he had a leaky valve in his heart which could have been the reason for the odd mistakes he used to make in some of his races. Mr Nesfield, who had been training for ten years, rode as an amateur and in 1956 had won the Lady Dudley Cup on Galloping Gold at the Worcestershire Hunt.

Tuesday 12 April	£1,392	Three miles and six furlongs
1 Kilburn (C. Nesfield)	8-11-2	Tim Norman
2 Cotswold (C.H. Davies)	7-10-2	S. Rooney
3 Jomsviking (R. Turnell)	9-11-2	J. King

Winning owner Madame Borel de Bitche

11 ran.   Distances: 3l, 5l, short head.   SP 11/4, 100/7, 2/1 fav.

Going heavy.

Kilburn, bay gelding by Battle Burn-Steel Point

1967

With Sorbus, a 9/2 chance, being withdrawn not under orders, only six horses faced the starter for the 1967 renewal of the Welsh Grand National. The seven-year-old Chilley Bridge, partnered by Bob Davies, made most of the running until four fences from home when Happy Spring, who has the distinction of being one of the very few horses to have beaten the mighty Arkle (he had divided Mill House and Arkle when second in the 1963 Hennessy Gold Cup), stayed on well in very deep going to win by four lengths from Pearlita with Comforting Wave third and a very tired Chilley Bridge in fourth place.

Pearlita had every chance two fences out, but couldn't quicken in the underfoot conditions. Happy Spring, who had jumped well throughout, was

Mrs Dorothy Wright with her 1967 Welsh Grand National winner Happy Spring.

confidently ridden by twenty-four-year-old Ken White – one of the strongest riders of his day. Backers of the favourite, Green Parrot, were as sick as the proverbial one when he fell at the second fence. Happy Spring was bred by Mrs Dorothy Wright and trained by her husband Stan at Bromyard, Herefordshire. Mr Wright claimed that Happy Spring was unlucky to have been around the same time as Arkle and Mill House, and there can be few who would disagree with him. Even so Happy Spring, who went on to win the inaugural Midlands Grand National at Uttoxeter, won ten chases during his racing career and these included the Rhymney Breweries Handicap Chase at Chepstow in 1962 and the Golden Miller Handicap Chase at Cheltenham in 1963.

Ken 'Stoker' White, who rode his first winner in 1959, was a great judge of pace. He will always be associated with Comedy Of Errors, on whom he won the Irish Sweeps Hurdle in 1974 and the Champion Hurdle in 1975. He also won the Scottish Champion Hurdle on two occasions with Coral Diver in 1972 and Comedy Of Errors in 1975 and in 1970 had won the Mackeson Gold Cup on Chatham. He hung up his riding boots in 1976 as a result of a recurring shoulder injury.

Tuesday 28 March	£1,392		Three miles and six furlongs
1 Happy Spring (J.S. Wright)	11-10-4	Ken White
2 Pearlita (R. Armytage)	8-10-12	C.Searle
3 Comforting Wave (G. Gregson)	10-9-12	P. Kelleway

Winning owner Mrs Dorothy Wright

6 ran.   Distances 4l,10l, bad.   SP 6/1, 9/2, 8/1.

Fav. Green Parott 3/1 (fell).   Going soft.

Happy Spring, bay gelding by Tambourin-Smart Woman

1968

Mrs Maxwell Joseph's seven-year-old chestnut Glenn outjumped his seven rivals to win this year's renewal. Glenn, who was thought to be a much better horse over two miles, won by four lengths from Fort Knight with the previous year's runner-up Pearlita a further neck away in third place. The Fossa, who like Glenn was trained by Fred Rimell, finished fourth.

Glenn's jockey, Eddie Harty told Pat Lucas, 'Glenn was prone to make one very bad mistake in a race, and for that reason I had to settle him down towards the rear of the field with plenty of light at his fences. As he was a horse with a lot of speed – a two-mile horse – the slower gallop over three miles and six furlongs gave him that bit longer to think and measure his fences. In this way, he gave the most superb jumping round one could wish for. It was solely his jumping that took him to the front at the third last. I never had to ask him for any real effort after that, and he won by four lengths from Fort Knight ridden by Stan Mellor.'

A former winning hurdler, Glenn won his first race over fences at Doncaster and would probably have won at the Cheltenham Festival but for falling three fences from the finish. He soon made amends by winning the Mildmay at Aintree and the following season won the Welsh Grand National. Sadly, three seasons later he was killed in a fall at Worcester. Harty, who went on to win the Aintree National the following season on Highland Wedding, had ridden his first winner under Rules fifteen years earlier. But before that he had ridden the winners of more than fifty Irish point-to-points. A true all-round horseman, he is the only man to have represented his country in the Olympic three-day event and to have ridden a Grand National winner. Another big steeplechase that went his way was the 1968 Mackeson Gold Cup which he won on Jupiter Boy.

Tuesday 16 April	£1,392	Three miles and six furlongs
1 Glenn (T.F. Rimell)	7-10-4	E.P. Harty
2 Fort Knight (P. Ransom)	9-9-7	S. Mellor
3 Pearlita (R. Armytage)	9-9-7	C. Searle

Winning owner Mr Maxwell Joseph
8 ran.   Distances: 4l, neck, 1½l.   SP 11/2, 9/2, 8/1.
Joint 3/1 favs. The Fossa (4th) and The Beeches (6th).   Going firm.
Glenn, chestnut gelding by Court Harwell-Solitaire

1970

In an effort to make the race more competitive, the Chepstow Executive moved the race from its traditional Easter time slot to late February. But this backfired somewhat when snow caused the 1969 Welsh Grand National to be abandoned. There were no problems though in 1970.

The favourite, Arctic Actress, who carried top weight of 10st 12lb, led to the nineteenth fence before fading rather quickly and leaving Astbury in the lead. Terry Biddlecombe riding the Fred Rimell trained French Excuse was with the leaders and going well when a bad mistake at the water jump appeared to put him out of the race.

Biddlecombe recalled, 'French Excuse was a very difficult horse, and a little bit thick in the wind. He landed in the water with me on the second circuit – he

Astbury (no. 10) leads French Excuse (no. 3) in the 1970 Welsh Grand National.

should have fallen really – and I didn't know whether to pull him up or not. I thought he might have hurt his back. Then I went on into the straight, gave him every chance to get his wind back, and after a right battle got up to win. French Excuse ran his guts out that day and never got over the race. I was exhausted, I had cramp, nearly collapsed in the weighing room, and I remember the doctor giving me a mixture of Guinness and salt, which was revolting!'

Astbury, who had been hard ridden in the closing stages, hit the last fence and was unable to quicken and although beaten by half-a-length by French Excuse managed to hold off Pride Of Kentucky for second place. China Cloed was a long way behind in fourth place. Unfortunately, shortly afterwards, twenty-nine-year-old Biddlecombe, who had been champion jockey on three occasions and had looked like being so again this season, had a fall at Kempton when his mount, King's Dream, stumbled on the flat and rolled on top of him. His injuries were so bad that he missed a winning ride on Gay Trip in the Grand National. There were few stronger riders in a finish than Biddlecombe who, during the course of his race-riding career, probably broke more bones than any other National Hunt jockey.

Saturday 21 February	**£3,314**		**Three miles and six furlongs**
1 French Excuse (T.F. Rimell)	8-10-9		Terry Biddlecome
2 Astbury (J. Bissill)	7-9-10		J. Bourke
3 Pride of Kentucky (E. Courage)	8-9-13		J. Buckingam

Winning owner Mr J.W. Jennings
11 ran.   Distances: ½l, ¾l, 2l.   SP 3/1, 100/7, 25/1.
Fav. Arctic Actress 11/4 (pulled up).   Going soft.
French Excuse, bay gelding by Alibi II-Ma Poupee (Le Sage)

1971

The going was hock deep in 1971 and Richard Pitman, now a BBC Television racing commentator, set out to make the pace on the seven-year-old Sandy Sprite. Having ridden Royal Toss to victory in the 1970 Whitbread Gold Cup, Pitman, knowing that Royal Toss was a notoriously careless jumper, planned to set an extremely fast gallop. This would put Royal Toss, the favourite, ridden by his brother-in-law, Paddy Cowley, under pressure in the hope that he would make some jumping mistakes and put himself out of the race. But to Pitman's dismay when he took a look over his shoulder on the turn for home the only horse he could see chasing him was the one he feared the most – Royal Toss. Royal Toss caught the weakening Sandy Sprite at the penultimate obstacle and went on to win by eight lengths to give 'Cowboy' Cowley his second success in

Mrs Handel leading in her 1971 Welsh Grand National winner Royal Toss with Paddy Cowley in the saddle.

the race. 'He was a very good horse with endless stamina and I knew Sandy Sprite would come back to us because of the going,' recalled Cowley, who had earned his nick name 'Cowboy' because, just like a rodeo rider, he often held the back of his saddle with one hand when taking a jump! Sadly, Cowley who later took up training horses after riding around 350 winners, the last of them in Norway at the age of forty-seven, died aged fifty-nine in 1992.

The following year Royal Toss, ridden by Nigel Wakley, finished runner-up to Glencaraig Lady in the Cheltenham Gold Cup beaten just three parts of a length. Paddy's son Simon Cowley remembered, 'Royal Toss was a pretty scary ride as a novice chaser, but Paddy got him going. Several of his colleagues had warned him he was going to hurt himself, but his persistence paid off. Sadly, and inexplicably, after his success in the Welsh Grand National Tim Handel, the trainer, told Paddy he would not ride the horse again. To his death Dad never knew why he was jocked off in this peremptory manner. Tim Handel never gave a reason.'

As a winner of the Whitbread Gold Cup, Mildmay, Mandarin and Gainsborough Gold Cups, Royal Toss, whose dam Spinning Coin II won eight open point-to-point races and two hunter chases, was surely one of the best horses ever to win the Welsh Grand National.

Saturday 20 February	£2,825	Three miles and six furlongs

1	Royal Toss (C.W.H. Handel)	9-10-12	Paddy Cowley
2	Sandy Sprite (J.A.C. Edwards)	7-10-2	R. Pitman
3	The Pantheon (T.F. Rimell)	8-10-13	T Biddlecombe

Winning owner Mr H. Handel

13 ran.   Distances: 8l, 30l, head.   SP 15/8 fav., 12/1, 7/1.   Going heavy.

Royal Toss, brown gelding by Royal Challenger-Spinning Coin II

1972

One of the biggest crowds in years witnessed one of the most popular wins in years when little Charlie H came home two-and-a-half-lengths clear of Fair Vulgan in the 1972 race. Owned jointly by Chepstow steward Johnny Clay, the former Glamorgan and England cricketer and Mrs Sue Williams, Charlie H was bought from Jim Joel who had ordered trainer Bob Turnell to sell him as he did not think he would amount to much. But the stylish thirty-one-year-old Johnnie Haine brought Charlie H with a bold run to take the lead from the front running Fair Vulgan at the second last fence to score a splendid victory. Foxtor was third and The Leap forth.

Mr Clay, a great supporter of National Hunt racing and a former point-to-point rider, admitted at the time that he was a little surprised at the result as he thought the horse was carrying a few pounds too much. However, a modest

Charlie H. lands the 1972 Welsh Grand National with Johnnie Haine aboard.

Johnnie Haine, who felt beforehand that he had a good chance of winning said, 'Sir Roger was going the best and would have won if he had stood up.' Sir Roger fell at the fourth last fence after he had just taken the lead from Fair Vulgan and his rider Swanny Haldane said, 'He hit the top of it otherwise I think I would have won.'

Johnnie Haine had more than one reason though to remember his Welsh Grand National success. Driving home after racing that evening his car left the road and was a write-off. And he hadn't even been celebrating! Haine, son-in-law of trainer Harry Thomson Jones, rode his first winner as a fifteen-year-old apprentice to Bob Turnell. He rode thirty winners on the Flat before switching to National Hunt racing and his notable triumphs included the Champion Hurdle, Scottish Grand National, Imperial Cup, Topham Trophy, Daily Express Triumph Hurdle and the Gloucester Hurdle on three occasions.

Charlie H's joint-owner, Mrs C.C. Williams, was later to become the first woman steward for National Hunt racing at Chepstow. She came from a very sporting family and her father, Mr R.H. Williams, was Master of the Glamorgan Hunt for twenty years. He was also a steward at Cardiff Racecourse. Mrs Williams had horses with Bob Turnell for more than twenty-five years perhaps the best of them being Tree Tangle.

Saturday 19 February	£3,286	Three miles and six furlongs
1 Charlie H (R. Turnell)	10-11-3	Johnnie Haine
2 Fair Vulgan (C. Bell)	8-10-3	M. Barnes
3 Foxtor (D. Barons)	8-11-6	B.R. Davies

Winning owners Mr J.C. Clay and Mrs C.C. Williams

9 ran.   Distances: 2½l, 4l, 15l.   SP 11/2, 7/1, 7/2 fav.   Going heavy.

Charlie H, bay gelding by Vulgan-Polly Roger

1973

Three-and-a-half inches of snow fell on Chepstow Racecourse during the week before the race – now known as the Corals Welsh Grand National with increased prize money of more than £2,000 – but it melted just in time for the race to take place. It was an exciting race with at least half-a-dozen of the sixteen starters battling it out for the lead going to the final fence.

It was a former point-to-pointer and hunter chaser that emerged victorious. Owned by Kidderminster permit holder George Yardley and beautifully ridden by twenty-one-year-old Nigel Wakley, Deblin's Green jumped the last just behind

Marshalla 'Taffy' Salaman who finished second on Sixer in the 1973 Welsh Grand National.

Sixer, who had been given a tremendous ride by Welshman 'Taffy' Salaman. It was then only in the last fifty yards that Deblin's Green surged ahead to score by a length. Vulkie finished third ahead of Persian Lark with the international singer Miss Dorothy Squires's Esban in fifth place. Ten leading jockeys were said to have turned down the ride on mudlark Deblin's Green and it was only at the eleventh hour, after a countrywide search, that Wakley, who was 8lbs over the 9st.7lb. he was set to carry, was contacted. He was rewarded with the then biggest win of his race riding career.

As for Deblin's Green, Pat Lucas, in her excellent book, *Fifty Years Of Racing At Chepstow*, has this to say, 'Deblin's Green had had two close brushes with death in his younger days. When he was first hunted, he slipped and crashed into a gate, gouging a hole in his head and losing so much blood it was a miracle he survived. Then, on joining his dam and her new foal at foot in a little escapade which led them on to the main road adjoining the farm, he was involved in an accident with a car and was so badly injured that he had to have

The 1973 runner-up Sixer with his owner/trainer Glynne Clay.

Deblin's Green holds off Sixer's challenge.

a hundred stitches in his belly. Throughout his career, which ended at Warwick when he shattered a foreleg, he bore the scars of those early misfortunes.'

The runner-up Sixer was owned and trained by Mr Glynne Clay, a son of Johnny Clay, who was to become Chairman of Chepstow Racecourse.

Saturday 17 February	£5,382	Three miles and six furlongs

1	Deblin's Green (G.H. Yardley)	10-9-12	Nigel Wakley
2	Sixer (G. Clay)	9-9-8	M. Salaman
3	Vulkie (L. Scott)	10-9-8	J. Nolan

Winning owner Mr G.H. Yardley

16 ran.   Distances: 1½l, 1½l.   SP 20/1, 16/1, 33/1.

Fav. Mocharabuice 11/4 (6th).

Deblin's Green, bay gelding by Pinicola-Pandy's Folly

1974

Hednesford trainer Earl Jones, who had saddled the 1962 winner Forty Secrets, won his second Welsh Grand National when Mr T. Winterton's Pattered, an eight-year-old son of Derby winner St Paddy, ploughed through the glue-pot going to win by four lengths from Deblin's Green who had put in a bold bid to win the race for the second successive year.

Pattered, under Ken 'Stoker' White, who had been successful on Happy Spring in 1967, jumped faultlessly throughout and had little difficulty in holding off Deblin's Green who had kept on at one pace to the line. A further three parts of a length away in third spot came Deck Steward, ridden by Vic Soane, while the 1972 Aintree National winner Well To Do made some late headway to finish fourth.

The early leaders were Deblin's Green and Sixer, with Interview II a faller at the first open ditch. Clever Scot took over as the field began to string out then suddenly the top weight dropped back and was eventually pulled up by David Mould. Despite being nearly unseated at the second open ditch, Even Dawn with Ron Hyett aboard moved up into third place, but from then on lost at least two lengths at each fence through deliberate jumping. With three fences to go Pattered and Deblin's Green battled it out, but a spectacular leap at the last by Pattered clinched it.

Earl Jones had every reason to be delighted with Pattered as it was his first winner in more than three months! The going was so desperate that of the twenty-four starters only ten of them completed the course. Pattered was a tough, brave and remarkable horse in more ways than one. Two months earlier, when a virus had raged through Earl Jones's yard, he had been a very sick horse indeed. Before the start, the astute Earl Jones had told Ken White to give Pattered a breather at around two-and-a-half miles so that the chestnut could get his second wind. White followed his instructions and landed the prize.

Saturday 16 February	£5,268		Three miles and six furlongs
1 Pattered (Earl Jones)	8-10-2	Ken White	
2 Deblin's Green (G.H. Yardley)	11-9-9	R. Smith	
3 Deck Steward (F. Winter)	8-10-3	V Soane	

Winning owner Mr T. Winterton

24 ran.   Distances: 4l, ¾l, 3l.   SP 25/1,14/1,25/1.

Fav. Clarification 11/2 (pulled up).   Going heavy.

Pattered, chestnut gelding by St Paddy-Mieux Rouge

1976

The 1975 race had unfortunately been abandoned owing to the course being waterlogged following torrential rain. In 1976, Jenny Pitman's promising Gylippus was made a 9/2 favourite in a field of seventeen runners and when the seven-year-old struck the front with a mile to go his backers started to search their pockets for their betting tickets. Gylippus's rider Bryan Smart, quickly extended his lead to some five lengths while Rag Trade, Man On The Moon and Even Up set off in pursuit with the rest well strung out. Gylippus still had a two lengths lead as he approached the final fence, but was clearly tiring and although horse and rider left the ground alright, Gylippus never reached high enough to clear the obstacle and catapulted Smart out of the saddle.

This enabled Johnny Burke on the Midlands Grand National winner Rag Trade to run out a two-and-a-half-lengths winner from the top weighted Even Up under Chris Read. Man On The Moon and Bob Champion took third place with Another Muddle fourth. Rag Trade was Fred Rimell's fourth Welsh Grand National winner as a trainer.

Gylippus falls at the last when leading the field in the 1976 race.

Bred in Ireland by Ian Williams, a son of former Welsh jockey Evan Williams, Rag Trade, a great big ten-year-old chestnut, was owned by 'Teasy Weasy' Raymond the flamboyant hairdresser. Rag Trade went on to win this year's Aintree National beating the legendary Red Rum and became the first horse to win the Welsh and English Grand Nationals since Cloister in 1896. Although it has to be admitted that Cloister won the Welsh equivalent three years after winning at Aintree.

Burke, aged twenty-three, who also partnered Rag Trade at Aintree the following month, later won the Cheltenham Gold Cup on Royal Frolic. He gave up riding in 1985 but while working for trainer Simon Christian in 1995 he had a heart attack from which he sadly died.

The 1975/76 season was a truly remarkable one for Fred Rimell as his horses set a stakes record by winning £111,740. This beat by some £10,000 the previous stakes best set by Fred Winter.

Rag Trade, following his Aintree National victory, was dogged with injuries and after two more attempts of a repeat success at Liverpool he broke down badly in the second of them and was subsequently put down.

Saturday 21 February	**£7,905**	**Three miles and six furlongs**	
1	Rag Trade (T.F. Rimell)	10-11-2	John Burke
2	Even Up (Mrs D. Oughton)	9-11-9	C. Read
3	Man On The Moon (J. Gifford)	7-10-6	R. Champion

Winning owner Mr P.B. Raymond

17 ran.   Distances: 2½l, 1½l, 20l.   SP 17/2, 12/1, 14/1.

Fav. Gylippus 9/2 (fell).

Rag Trade, chestnut gelding by Menelek-The Rage

1979

With the 1977 race abandoned owing to the course being waterlogged and the 1978 race called off owing to frost it was no real surprise to find that the 1979 race, held as usual in February, was abandoned owing to snow. However, with the Jockey Club granting permission for the Chepstow executive to change the month of the race to December for future events, the 1979 race went ahead as planned on the new date granted which was 22 December.

David Gandolfo's eight-year-old Peter Scot was given a good ride by twenty-five year old Paul Barton in this year's renewal. In a handy position throughout, Peter Scot went clear at the eighteenth fence and ran on under pressure to beat Current Gold, ridden by Jonjo O'Neil, by four lengths. Prince Rock ran his usual good race to finish a further five lengths back under Ron Barry to take third place from Master Smudge the subsequent Cheltenham Gold Cup winner. A well beaten fifth was Gyllipus who had fallen at the last in 1976. The joint favourites, Jack Madness and Chumsun, both failed to complete the course. Jack Madness unseated his rider at the last and Chumsun was brought down at the eighth.

Peter Scot, the 1979 Welsh Grand National winner.

Third Race.
DAILY DOUBLE

About Three Miles, Six Furlongs, for Five Yrs Old and Upwards

1.50 The Coral Welsh National (Handicap Steeple Chase)
£17,500 added to stakes
Distributed in accordance with Rule 194(Iv)(a)
(includes a fourth prize)
for five yrs old and upwards
about THREE MILES, SIX FURLONGS
£25 to enter,

WP.

3m6F £50 extra unless forfeit declared by .... November 27th
£50 extra if declared to run
Penalties, after November 14th, a winner of a steeple chase
value £3000 .... 6lb
Half penalties for horses originally handicapped at or above 11st 7lb
The Horserace Betting Levy Board Prize Money Scheme provides for
the inclusion of £3000 in the added money subscribed for this race
CORAL RACING LTD. have generously given £10,500 included in the
value of this Pattern race
A trophy value £750 is included in the value of this race
*The Stewards of the Jockey Club have modified Rule 121(ii)(a) for
the purpose of this race*

102 entries, 32 at £25, 50 at £75 and 20 at £125.—Closed November
7th, 1979.

Owners Prize Money. Winner £11,794; Second £4048; Third £1961;
Fourth £918
(Penalty Value £15,832.50)

Form			Trainer	Age st lb	
331-112 C	**2**	CHUMSON (NZ) .... 8 11 4 ...... Br g Sobig (NZ)—Gay Amber Mr R. S. Donald (F. T. Winter, Lambourn) ORANGE, WHITE sleeves and cap, MAUVE armlets			J. Francome
12-1330	**3**	MASTER SMUDGE .... 7 11 0 ...... Ch g Master Stephen—Lily-Pond II Mr A. Barrow (A. Barrow, Bridgwater) LIGHT BLUE, RED diamond, qtd cap			R. Hoare
F020-31 C-D	**4**	PRINCE ROCK .... 11 10 12 ...... B g Autre Prince—Roxana III Mr Michael Buckley (P. G. Bailey, Wantage) Mr F. R. Watts BLACK and WHITE qtd, sleeves reversed, check cap			R. Barry
F0-2111	**5**	JACK MADNESS .... 7 10 6 ...... (in 6lb ex) Bl or br g David Jack—Tarby Mr Peter Hopkins (J. T. Gifford, Findon) Mr S. Lanaway ORANGE, WHITE chevrons on body, WHITE cap			R. Rowe
1311-14 C	**7**	LOCHAGE .... 8 10 3 ...... B g Spartan General—Queen of the Jungle Major A. K. Barlow (Capt. T. A. Forster, Wantage) YELLOW, BLACK spots and sleeves, WHITE cap			J. King
10200-1	**8**	PETER SCOT .... 8 10 2 ...... B g Jock Scot—Miss Peter Mr G. E. Amey (D. R. Gandolfo, Wantage) Mr R. W. Amey GREEN, WHITE cross-belts, NAVY BLUE sleeves and cap			P. Barton

(Continued next page.)

CORAL WELSH NATIONAL (HANDICAP STEEPLE CHASE)—continued.

Form			Trainer	Age st lb	
4P0-134	**9**	CURRENT GOLD .... 8 10 1 ...... Ch g Current Coin—Souvergold Mr A. M. Picken (G. W. Richards, Penrith) MAROON, GOLD sash and cap with MAROON spots			J. J. O'Neil
3C-1103	**10**	GOOD PROSPECT .... 10 10 1 ...... Br g Orchardist—Lagini's Plumage Mrs J. A. C. Edwards (J. A. C. Edwards, Ross-on-Wye) Mr A. S. Robinson YELLOW, PURPLE hooped sleeves, RED cross-belts			S. Morshead
1111-P3	**12**	SPARKLING TARQUA .... 8 10 0 ...... Ch m Never Die Dancing—Lucrece Mr W. James (W. James, Taunton) YELLOW, BLACK sash and cap with WHITE spots			P. Warner
2000-41 C-D	**13**	DEIOPEA .... 8 10 0 ...... Ch m Spartan General—Woodland Wedding Mr Mark Stephens (M. Stephens, Taunton) DEEP PURPLE, LILAC cross-belts and hoop on cap			S. C. Knight
F-F0333	**14**	RED EARL .... 10 10 0 ...... B g Sunny Way—Mary Scott Mr Henry Ford (J. Berry, Cockerham) YELLOW, NAVY BLUE and RED hooped sleeves and qtd cap			
FP-3F22	**15**	PRINCELY BID .... 8 10 0 ...... B g Raise You Ten—Leney Princess Sir John Thomson (R. C. Armytage, East Ilsley) WHITE, ORANGE hoop, qtd cap			H. Davies
001F1-0	**16**	GYLIPPUS .... 10 10 0 ...... Ch g Spartan General—Rainbow Battle Mr Tony Stratton Smith (Mrs J. Pitman, Upper Lambourn) MAUVE, EMERALD GREEN sleeves, RED cap			S. Smith Eccles
422F20-	**17**	ROYAL SPLASH .... 10 10 0 ...... B g Royal Record II—Air Sil Mrs H. I. Houlbrooke (Mrs H. I. Houlbrooke, Ledbury) MAGENTA, BLACK sleeves, GREEN cap			Mr T. Houlbrooke
000/PP0	**18**	BARROW CHIEF .... 10 10 0 ...... Br g Indian Ruler—Averona Mr L. Morse (O. O'Neill, Cheltenham) MAROON, WHITE stripe and spots on cap			
0-20241	**20**	MRS STEPHENS .... 9 10 0 ...... B or br m Master Stephen—Dreamless Mrs M. A. T. Potter (K. Lewis, St Clears) CERISE, GOLD sleeves and spots on cap			P. Barry

NUMBER OF DECLARED RUNNERS 16 (DUAL FORECAST)

RIDERS' ALLOWANCES
RED Number on WHITE Board indicates 7lb taken. BLACK Number on
ORANGE Board indicates 4lb taken.

Racecard entries for the 1979 Welsh Grand National.

The win came as something of a surprise for winning owner Graham Amey whose late mother, Phylis Amey, had bred Peter Scot. He reminisced, 'It was a bitterly cold day and trainer David Gandolfo, who was at another meeting, was represented by his wife, Anna. We were watching the race from the grandstand with my eleven-year-old son, Thomas who was so cold that he was stamping his feet and clapping his hands to keep warm. Then Anna started jumping up and down, but not to ward off the cold. She could see that our horse was winning and was getting excited!' Mr Amey added, 'It was certainly a day I shall never forget.'

Saturday 22 December	**£15,832**	**Three miles and six furlongs**

1	Peter Scot (D. Gandolfo)	8-10-2	Paul Barton
2	Current Gold (G.W. Richards)	8-10-1	J.J. O'Neil
3	Prince Rock (P. Bailey)	11-10-12	R. Barry

Winning owner Mr Graham Amey

15 ran. Distances: 4l, 5l, 3l. SP 8/1, 15/2, 8/1. Jt.favs. 9/2 Jack Madness
(unseated rider) and Chumson (brought down). Going soft.

Peter Scot, bay gelding by Jock Scot-Miss Peter

1980

Newport housewife Linda Sheedy, a mother of twin boys, made a little bit of racing history when finishing in tenth and last place in this year's race on Deiopea. Linda was the first female jockey to take part in the race. She can also claim to be the first woman to have ridden in the Cheltenham Gold Cup and there cannot be many jockettes who can boast of having ridden in the English, Scottish and Welsh Grand Nationals. Linda was also the first Welsh woman jockey to ride a winner over-the-sticks when the rules of racing were first changed to allow women to compete against men.

Noel Crump, who had trained the 1951 winner Skyreholme, watched the 1980 Coral Welsh Grand National on television from the press room at Doncaster. He was delighted when his seven-year-old Narvic, who had run so indifferently in his previous outing at Haydock, ran out a comfortable eight lengths winner from Prince Rock who had finished third the previous year. Narvic, ridden for the first time by one of steeplechasing's greatest jockeys John Francome, made most of the running. He dashed ahead of his pursuers entering the straight and despite pecking at the penultimate fence ran on well for his stylish pilot.

In third place, a further four lengths behind, came Jenny Pitman's Artistic Prince while the previous year's winner, Peter Scot, who had lost touch after half-way, was pulled up approaching the last fence. The favourite, Silent Valley, partnered by Peter Scudamore, blundered away his chances and was pulled up before the seventeenth fence.

Master Smudge, who finished fourth, three months later ran in the Cheltenham Gold Cup and was an eight lengths runner-up to the Irish-trained Tied Cottage. However, Tied Cottage was subsequently disqualified in controversial circumstances for failing a dope test and the race awarded to Master Smudge.

Narvic was something of a temperamental character who often raced in blinkers. Even so he won twelve chases the last of them at Warwick. John Francome, aged twenty-eight, started his riding career in gymkhanas and became a British show-jumping international in 1969. He had ridden Midnight Court to land the 1978 Cheltenham Gold Cup and in 1981 was successful in the Champion Hurdle on Sea Pigeon. From 5,072 mounts he rode 1,138 winners and was champion jockey no fewer than seven times. He was awarded the MBE in 1986 and is now a Channel 4 television racing commentator and author.

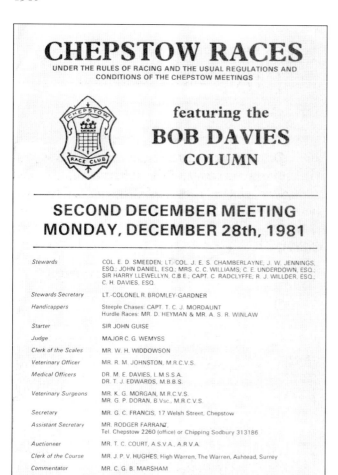

Chepstow Racecard, 1981.

Saturday 20 December   **£15,458**   **Three miles and six furlongs**

---

1 Narvic (N. Crump)   7-10-11   John Francome
2 Prince Rock (P. Bailey)   12-10-9   B.R. Davies
3 Artistic Prince (Mrs J. Pitman)   9-10-2   B.Smart

Winning owner Lady Cadogan
18 ran.   Distances: 8l, 4l, 12l.   SP 15/1,13/1,14/1.
Fav. 5/1 Silent Valley (pulledup).   Going heavy.
Narvic, bay gelding by Star Moss-Kerstina

1981

It took the connections of Peaty Sandy ten-and-a half hours to travel the 300 miles from Innerleithen in Scotland to Chepstow for the 1981 race. But it was a journey that paid handsome dividends. Little Peaty Sandy, unpenalised for two runaway wins after the weights were published, took up the running from the pacemaking Prince Rock at the eighteenth fence to score a convincing ten lengths win from Royal Russe, with Prince Rock in third and Colonel Christy in fourth place.

Linda Sheedy, riding the seventeen hands high Foxbury, finished a creditable seventh of the twenty-three starters.

Welshman Hywel Davies, who went on to win the 1985 Aintree Grand National on Last Suspect, could only finish fifth on Shady Deal in this year's Welsh Grand National. Photo by Carl Burrows.

Welsh jockey Dai Tegg finished eighth on Jeff King's Pelion in 1988.

Peaty Sandy, a tough, genuine stayer, was ridden by the smart amateur rider Geordie Dun, who missed his Christmas dinner to put up only 3lbs. overweight after managing to shed some 7lbs. The runner-up, Royal Russe, was owned by George Yardley who was more than happy with the result. Owing to the bad weather his mare hadn't had a gallop since winning over the course three weeks earlier. Mr Yardley, it will be remembered, had won the 1973 Welsh Grand National with Deblin's Green.

Monday 28 December	**£18,505**		**Three miles and six furlongs**
1 Peaty Sandy (Miss H. Hamilton)	7-10-3		Mr T.G. Dun
2 Royal Russe (G.H. Yardley)	8-9-10		P. Carvill
3 Prince Rock (P. Bailey)	13-10-1		P. Scudamore

Winning owner Miss H. Hamilton

23 ran.   Distances: 10l, 25l, 12l.   SP 3/1 fav., 9/1,12/1.   Going soft.

Peaty Sandy, bay gelding by Spartan General-Petlow

1982

Mr Bryan Burrough's seven-year-old, well-bred Corbiere came with a storming late run under twenty-two-year-old Ben de Haan, who was riding his first big race winner. Corbiere beat Pilot Officer by a head with the previous year's winner Peaty Sandy a well beaten third ahead of the odds-on favourite, Captain John who had led from the thirteenth to the eighteenth fence, but eventually had trailed in fourth after pulling a muscle in his back.

The following year, 1983, Corbiere went on to win the real thing at Aintree and his two thirds – carrying 12st in 1984 and 11st 10lb in 1985 – must surely make him one of the best Grand National horses since the days of Red Rum.

Son of that very good hurdler Harwell, out of the maiden Ballycashin – a sister or half-sister to several winners – Corbiere was giving 10lb to the runner-up whose rider, Sam Morshead, apparently acting under orders, objected that the winner had taken his ground on the run-in. The stewards, however, quickly dismissed his complaint confiscating Morshead's £30 deposit and fined him another £30 for making a frivolous objection.

Corbiere, or to give him his stable name 'Corky', was trained by Jenny Pitman who had looked like winning the race six years earlier when Gylippus had been a last fence faller. For the first time in the history of the race, the first three home were all saddled by women trainers. The runner up, Pilot Officer, was trained by Mercy Rimell and the third, Peaty Sandy, by Helen Hamilton.

Ben de Haan, who I believe has Welsh connections on his mother's side, had ridden his first winner at Chepstow a couple of seasons earlier on Arctic Princess. He was to ride Corbiere to victory in the 1983 Aintree National, the first time the world's greatest steeplechase had been won by a woman trainer and he also has a Norwegian 'Grand National' win to his credit. He now trains at Lambourn in Berkshire.

Jenny Pitman had certainly made a name for herself in the world of steeplechasing since I had visited her yard some years earlier when she had trained a point-to-pointer called The Rabbi for two friends of mine Tony Harris and Tom Griffiths. Her training days behind her, she is now an author of novels with a racing background.

Racing scribe Brian Lee (left) with Chepstow Racecourse manager Rodger Farrant, Chepstow Racecourse, 1993.

Tuesday 28 December	£16,321	Three miles and six furlongs

1   Corbiere (Mrs Jenny Pitman)   7-10-10   Ben de Haan
2   Pilot Officer (Mrs M. Rimell)   7-10-0   S. Morshead
3   Peaty Sandy (Miss H. Hamilton)   8-10-13   T.G. Dun

Winning owner Mr Bryan Burrough
9 ran.   Distances: head, 20l, 12l.   SP 12/1, 12/1, 9/4.
Fav 8/11. Captain John (4th).   Going soft.
Corbiere, chestnut gelding by Harwell-Bally Cashen

1983

Leading lady trainer Jenny Pitman, who had won the previous year's race with Corbiere, laid her reputation as a good judge of form on the line when the weights for the 1983 Welsh Grand National were published by declaring that, 'There was no way Burrough Hill Lad could get beaten.' She was that confident she told all her owners to help themselves to the ante-post odds of 20/1 that were available and a sustained gamble on the jet black horse saw him go to the post a 100/30 favourite.

Although the great John Francome had to put up 3lb overweight, Burrough Hill Lad, who was jumping fences in public for the first time in twelve months, came home a very easy winner from Royal Judgement who had made most of the running. Lucky Vane, under John Burke, was a further three lengths away with Mid Day Gun in fourth.

Corbiere had been prominent until weakening at the seventeenth and finished a distant sixth. Francome, who was riding the horse for the first time, had rode a patient race before tackling the top weighted Royal Judgement and on the run to the last he even had time to look around for non-existent dangers.

Burrough Hill Lad, who throughout most of his racing career was dogged with injuries, was bred by his owner, the Leicester restaurateur, Robert Stanley Riley. Being by Richboy out of Green Monkey, Burrough Hill Lad, named after the hills above Mr Riley's old farm, was really bred for the flat. Instead he went on to win, among other races, the 1984 Cheltenham Gold Cup, Hennessy Cognac Gold Cup and the King George VI Chase. Had he stayed sound there is no telling how many other big races this courageous, long striding powerhouse of a horse would have won.

Tuesday 27 December	£19,964		Three miles and six furlongs
1 Burrough Hill Lad (Mrs J. Pitman)	7-10-9	John Francome	
2 Royal Judgement (J. Gifford)	10-11-7	R. Rowe	
3 Lucky Vane (G.B. Balding)	8-10-5	J. Burke	

Winning owner Mr Robert Stanley Riley

18 ran.   Distances: 4l, 3l, 15l.   SP 100/30 fav., 25/1, 5/1.   Going soft.

Burrough Hill Lad, brown gelding by Richboy-Green Monkey

Monica Dickinson's pair Planetman and Righthand Man, both winners of their previous races, started first and second favourites for this year's race.

Planetman, who had been backed from 7/1, started a 4/1 favourite and Righthand Man was returned at odds of 6/1. Confidently ridden by twenty-four-year-old Graham Bradley, who had won the previous year's Cheltenham Gold Cup on Bregawn, Righthand Man was prominent from the start. Making light of his heavy weight in this severe test of stamina he drew clear at the penultimate fence to score by seven lengths from Lucky Vane with stable companion Planetman a further three lengths away in third place. Tacroy finished fourth.

Planetman had jumped well and was holding a useful looking lead until he made a mistake at the fourth fence from home where his pilot, Robert Earnshaw, had to work wonders to keep the partnership intact. Afterwards he claimed that the mistake had cost him the race and Mrs Dickinson was inclined to agree with him. But it has to be said that Righthand Man appeared to have plenty in hand at the finish and had run on well without being asked to change into top gear.

Peaty Sandy, winner in 1981, finished sixteenth and last after making a mistake at the second fence which he never recovered from. Of the eighteen starters, the only two horses who failed to complete the course were A Kinsman and Northern Bay who both fell in the closing stages of the race.

Despite finishing runner-up in both the Cheltenham Gold Cup and the Scottish Grand National, Righthand Man was never really the same horse again. He eventually succumbed to a viral infection of the lung and failing to respond to treatment was sadly put down in 1987.

Graham Bradley, one of National Hunt's controversial characters, rode his first winner at Sedgefield in 1980 and his last at Haydock in 1999. When he retired he wrote his autobiography *The Wayward Lad* which was a best seller.

Saturday 22 December   £19,132   Three miles and six furlongs

1	Righthand Man (Mrs M. Dickinson)	7-11-5	Graham Bradley
2	Lucky Vane (G.B. Balding)	9-11-2	J. Burke
3	Planetman (Mrs M. Dickinson)	7-10-0	R. Earnshaw

Winning owner Mrs M.M. Haggas

18 ran.   Distances: 7l, 3l, 1½l.   SP 6/1,13/2, 4/1 fav.   Going soft.

Righthand Man, bay gelding by Proverb-Gleann Buide (Pampered King)

1985

Run And Skip, a seven-year-old bay gelding, trained by forty-five-year-old John Spearing, made every yard of the running in the heavy going to win in 1985. Ridden with great confidence by Peter Scudamore, Run And Skip finished six lengths ahead of the 100/1 outsider Golden Ty with Kumbi third and the previous year's winner Righthand Man, under top weight of 11st 7lb, back in fourth place.

Scudamore, whose father Michael had won the race in 1957 on Creeola II, was originally down to ride Jenny Pitman's Smith's Man who was pulled up in the straight. Luckily for him, he changed his mind and teamed up with the winner instead.

Run And Skip, winner of the 1985 Welsh Grand National.

Run And Skip's win was the biggest success yet for the modest and quietly spoken Spearing who had been training horses at Alcester since 1971. A former amateur rider, he said in the unsaddling enclosure after the race that the horse had improved a great deal at home the fortnight before the race. Spearing added that he was confident four fences from home that the horse would not be caught.

The only hard luck story in my view belonged to Jonjo O'Neil who had a crashing fall from Broadheath who appeared to be going well when falling five fences from home.

It is interesting to note that among the also-rans were Peaty Sandy (5th), the 1983 Aintree National hero West Tip (6th), Corbiere (7th) and Rhyme 'N'Reason, (pulled up) who went on to win at Aintree in 1988.

Run And Skip, who was to finish fourth in the 1986 Cheltenham Gold Cup, was owned by Mr Walid Marzouk from Stoke Poges, a thirty-year-old businessman who dealt in marketing medical equipment.

Saturday 21 December	**£21,260**	**Three miles and six furlongs**

1	Run And Skip (J.L. Spearing)	7-10-8	Peter Scudamore
2	Golden Ty (G.V. Hall)	7-9-11	Mr A. Orkney
3	Kumbi (D. McCain)	10-10-3	S. Smith Eccles

Winning owner Mr Walid Marzouk

18 ran.   Distances: 6l, 2l, 1l.   SP 13/1, 100/1, 18/1.

Joint favourites 5/1 Planetman (9th) and Righthand Man (4th).   Going soft.

Run And Skip, bay gelding by Deep Run-Skiporetta (Even Money)

1986

Jenny Pitman saddled her third Coral Welsh National winner in five years when Stearsby, who was giving weight to all except I Haventalight, finished six lengths clear of stablemate Macoliver. In fact, she almost made it a 1-2-3 as her other representative, Corbiere, came in fourth beaten only by half-a-length for third place by M.H. Easterby's Jimbrook.

Graham Bradley moved up Stearsby to dispute the lead with the tiring Kumbi and Corbiere turning out of the back straight and was clear and going well when he made a slight mistake at the third last. Undaunted however, Stearsby stayed on well in the soft ground to score an impressive win for his owner Terry Ramsden. 'I had a great ride from him', exclaimed Bradley adding, 'He was going wonderfully well down the back straight and although he was tiring a little he kept going grand.'

Stearsby, who had been a rather erratic jumper in his novice chasing days, before he was trained by Jenny Pitman, was a lucky chance ride for Bradley due to Graham McCourt, who was retained to ride all of Mr Ramsden's horses, being in the middle of a twenty-eight-day riding suspension.

A big, workmanlike black horse, who always looked a picture in the parade ring, Stearsby won with 11st 5lbs. Only one other horse, Righthand Man, in the 1984 race, had carried that much weight since Limonali had won in 1961 with 11st 12lbs. Stearsby, who had been alarmingly fearless in his younger days, never fell when schooling but made such big holes in his fences that according to Jenny Pitman, 'You could have driven a tractor through.'

Bradley, who it will be recalled won the 1989 race on Righthand Man, carried on race riding for another thirteen years riding lots more winners.

Saturday 20 December	£21,136	Three miles and six furlongs
1 Stearsby (Mrs J. Pitman)	7-11-5	Graham Bradley
2 Macoliver (Mrs J. Pitman)	8-10-0	M. Perrett
3 Jimbrook (M.H. Easterby)	9-10-12	L. Wyer

Winning owner Mr Terry Ramsden

17 ran.   Distances: 6l, ½l, 3l.   SP 8/1,16/1, 14/1.   Fav. 9/2 Corbiere 4th.

Going soft.

Stearsby, black gelding by Politico (USA)-Lucky Sprite (Galivanter)

1987

The outstanding novice chaser Kildimo was backed from 5/1 to 3/1 favourite to land the 1987 Coral Welsh National. But he was never going well and trailed in ninth of the eleven finishers.

Midnight Madness, ridden by Mark Richards, made most of the early running in the testing ground before Little Polvier and Greenbank Park fought out the lead. On the turn to the home straight, Playschool, partnered by twenty-five year-old Paul Nicholls and Rhyme'N'Reason, under Ross Arnott, were on the heels of the leaders and soon had the race between them. Hard ridden in the closing stages, the New Zealand-bred Playschool held on to his narrow lead and Nicholls, asking his mount for a big one at the last, got it and had a length to spare at the winning post. Midnight Madness took third spot ahead of Dart Over.

'He's as game as hell, tries for ever and stays all day' said Nicholls on dismounting in the winner's enclosure. While Arnott, who rode into the place reserved for the runner up, volunteered, 'I think I should have kicked sooner in the straight as Playschool beat me for speed.'

Playschool was made favourite for the 1988 Cheltenham Gold Cup but was well behind when pulled up by Paul Nicholls who reported that, 'Something was seriously wrong.' Rumours circulated that the horse had been got at, but an official Jockey Club post-race dope test proved negative. Even so, Playschool's trainer, David Barons, remained convinced that somehow or other someone had got at his horse.

Rhyme'N'Reason went on to win the 1988 Aintree National and as for Nicholls, when he hung up his riding boots, he took out a trainers' licence and won the Cheltenham Gold Cup in 1999 with ex-point-to-pointer See More Business. He has been ranked number forty in the top fifty National Hunt trainers of all time which really says it all.

Playschool and Paul Nicholls who won the 1987 Welsh Grand National.

Monday 28 December   **£21,091**   **Three miles and six furlongs**

1	Playschool (D. Barons)	9-10-11	Paul Nicholls
2	Rhyme'N'Reason (D. Elsworth)	8-10-0	R. Arnott
3	Midnight Madness (D. Bloomfield)	9-10-1	M. Richards

Winning owner Mr R.E. Cottle

13 ran.   Distances: 1l, 25l, 1l, 1½l.   SP 5/1, 4/1, 25-1.

Fav. 3/1 Kildimi (9th).   Going soft, heavy in parts.

Playschool, bay gelding by Valuta-Min Tide (Harleigh)

1988

Five days before the weights for this year's race were published, the former smart hurdler Bonanza Boy won for his new trainer, Martin Pipe, at Newton Abbot. He trounced the more than useful Broadheath by twenty lengths. No wonder Pipe, who this season was to set a record for the fastest 100 winners ever trained in a season said, 'I told everyone that if you could ever have a good thing for the Welsh National then this is it.'

Even though little Bonanza Boy had to carry 7lb more than his long handicap weight he was still let off lightly and those punters who took the ante-post odds of 10/1 that were available had good cause to be pleased with themselves.

There were twelve starters and in the usual heavy conditions, the 1985 winner Run And Skip led to the nineteenth fence. Peter Scudamore, however, had Bonanza Boy in a handy position throughout and taking the lead early in the long straight soon went clear. Although Bonanza Boy jumped deliberately at times there was no real danger to him and he went on to score easily by twelve lengths from Run And Skip. The 1987 Cheltenham Gold Cup winner The Thinker, under top weight of 11st 10lb, finished a very leg weary third with Border Lad fourth.

Bonanza Boy was the second leg of a Scudamore/Pipe four-timer their three other Chepstow winners being Enemy Action, Fu's Lady and Elegant Isle.

Tuesday 27 December	£21,817		Three miles and six furlongs
1 Bonanza Boy (M. Pipe)	7-10-1	Peter Scudamore	
2 Run And Skip (J.L. Spearing)	10-10-3	G. McCourt	
3 The Thinker (W.A. Stephenson)	10-11-10	A. Merrigan	

Winning owner Mr S. Dunster

12 ran.   Distances: 12l, 25l, 8l.   SP 9/4 fav., 15/2,9/2.   Going soft.

Bonanza Boy, bay gelding by Sir Lark-Vulmid (Vulgan)

1989

Martin Pipe's Bonanza Boy made Welsh Grand National history in 1989 by becoming the first dual winner to win in successive years. The last dual winner Limonali had won in 1959 and 1961 while three times winner Lacatoi had been successful in 1935, 1937 and 1939. The only other dual winners – Razorbill had won in 1908 and 1911 and Miss Balscadden in 1926 and 1928 – had to wait three and two years respectively before winning the race a second time.

Backers of Bonanza Boy, who started a 15/8 favourite, must have been a little bit worried when on the first circuit he could be seen scratching along in mid division as Stearsby and Remedy The Malady led the field a merry dance on ground that could only be described as stamina sapping.

However, Bonanza Boy's jockey, Peter Scudamore, whose motto was 'never say die', didn't give up the chase and gradually eased his way to the leaders. Six fences from the finish, disaster nearly struck as Bonanza Boy, who was not much bigger than a polo pony, was badly hampered by the fall of Remedy The Malady which caused him to swerve and lose six or seven lengths. Undeterred, Bonanza Boy galloped on through the mud and taking the lead approaching the fourth last fence he went on to win by fifteen lengths from Cool Ground who beat Charter Hardware by half-a-length for second place. Ghofar finished fourth. Little Polvier, who ten months earlier had won the Aintree National, looked as though he needed the race and struggled home in seventh and last place.

Saturday 23 December	£21,980		Three miles and six furlongs
1 Bonanza Boy (M. Pipe)	8-11-11	Peter Scudamore	
2 Cool Ground (N.R. Mitchell)	7-9-13	A. Tory	
3 Charter Hardware (J.A.C Edwards)	7-9-11	N. Williamson	

Winning owner Mr S. Dunster

12 ran.   Distances: 15l, ½l, 4l.   SP 15/8 fav., 10/1, 9/1.   Going soft.

Bonanza Boy, bay gelding by Sir Lark-Vulmid (Vulcan)

1990

Thirty years before, in 1960, the Welsh Grand National had been won by a mare, Clover Bud, who had started her racing career on the Welsh point-to-point circuit. This year it was the turn of a former Irish point-to-pointer the leggy Cool Ground. Laid out specially for the race by Reg Akehurst, and jumping perfectly all the way round under Luke Harvey, Cool Ground, the eight-year-old son of the French-bred Over The River, drew clear three fences from home to win by seven lengths. He beat the 2/1 favourite Carrick Hill Lad, ridden by Welshman Neale Doughty from Kenfig Hill near Bridgend, who in 1984 had won the Aintree National on Hallo Dandy.

The one-paced Rowlandsons Jewells finished a further fifteen lengths back in third place with Yahoo a close fourth. Runner-up in the previous year's race, when trained by Richard Mitchell, Cool Ground was targeted for this race when Akehurst took over from Mitchell at Peter Barton's multi-million pound yard in Dorset six months or so earlier. Harvey's orders had been not to hit the front too soon, 'But he was going so well straightening for home I had to go on', said a jubilant Harvey. But Cool Ground's finest hour was still to come for two years later, when trained by Toby Balding and ridden by former leading Irish point-to-point champion rider Adrian Maguire, Cool Ground, a 25/1 outsider, landed the Cheltenham Gold Cup.

Dual winner Bonanza Boy was never going well and was pulled up approaching the sixteenth fence. The stewards ordered a routine dope test which proved negative.

For twenty-four-year-old Harvey the 1990/91 season was his best yet as he rode 42 winners all told.

Luke Harvey on his way to winning the 1990 race on Cool Ground.

Saturday 22 December	£22,958	Three miles and six furlongs

1 Cool Ground (R. Akehurst) — 8-10-0 — Luke Harvey
2 Carrick Hill Lad (G.W. Richards) — 7-10-11 — N. Doughty
3 Rowlandsons Jewels (D. Murray-Smith) — 9-10-2 — G. Bradley

Winning owner (Whitcombe Manor Racing Stables)
14 ran.   Distances 7l, 15l, ¾l.   SP 9/2, 2/1 fav., 25/1.
Going good, with soft patches.
Cool Ground, chestnut gelding by Over The River-Merry Spring (Merrymount)

1991

Top weight Carvill's Hill, shouldering a hefty 11st 12lb, left his sixteen rivals trailing in his wake when winning the 1991 renewal by twenty lengths from Party Politics who to frank the form four months later, went on to win the Aintree National with West Walian Carl Llewellyn aboard.

In winning Wales's most famous horse race, Carvill's Hill, who made all the running under Peter Scudamore, put up the finest weight-carrying performance since Limonali, who carrying the same weight, had been victorious thirty years earlier. Scudamore, who was winning the race for the fourth time, gave Carvill's Hill a breather at around half-way which allowed Esha Ness to get within half-a dozen lengths or so, but he drew clear again to score a resounding victory.

Carvill's Hill's trainer, Martin Pipe, who also trained the third horse Aquilifer and the fourth Bonanza Boy, said of the Irish-import, 'Carvill's Hill is the best horse I have ever trained. Scudamore went off so fast I thought he had forgotten it was two laps at Chepstow. But he rode a terrific race.' The giant Carvill's Hill had arrived from Ireland with a frustrating history of erratic jumping and back injuries and Pipe, surrounded by a dozen or so racing scribes, of which I was one, said, 'All the credit of sorting out Carvill's Hill's troubles must go to my backroom boys that have put in endless hours on the horse.'

A last-minute decision to run him at Chepstow in preference to the King George V at Kempton Park five days later gave record breaking Scudamore a fourth win in the race equalling Jack Fawcus's four-timer at Cardiff's Ely Racecourse in the 1930s.

Hailed by many as the next Arkle, Carvill's Hill sadly flopped in a controversial Cheltenham Gold Cup. It was suggested that Jenny Pitman's 150/1 chance Golden Freeze had been put in the race as a stalking horse to disrupt Carvill's Hill who, after making a first fence blunder, finished a distant last of five. It was later reported that Carvill's Hill had pulled muscles in his chest and back and a Jockey Club inquiry cleared Golden Freeze's connections of any wrongdoings.

Welshman Dai Burchell, who pulled up on Chief Ironside in the 1991 race.

Saturday 21 December	£23,654	Three miles and six furlongs

1	Carvill's Hill (M. Pipe)	9-11-12	Peter Scudamore
2	Party Politics (N. Gaslee)	7-10-7	A. Adams
3	Aquilifer (M. Pipe)	11-10-9	R. Dunwoody

Winning owner Mr Paul Green

17 ran.   Distances: 20l, short head, 20l.   SP 9/4 fav., 7/2, 8/1.

Going good to soft, soft patches.

Carvill's Hill, bay gelding by Roselier-Suir Valley (Orchardist)

1992

In this year's race, held on the Monday after Christmas before a huge holiday crowd, Martin Pipe's four runners finished an unprecedented 1-2-3-4. Run For Free, who had earned his stable lad £75 for winning the best turned out award, made all the running under thirty-year-old Mark Perrett who survived a bad blunder at the sixteenth fence that would have shot most other jockeys out of the saddle. The least fancied of Pipe's quartet, the 50/1 chance Riverside Boy who was second or third throughout, never looked like catching the appropriately named winner who had a good eight lengths to spare at the winning post. Joint favourite with Run For Free was the one-paced Miinnehoma who plodded on to take third place and former dual winner Bonanza Boy ran on gamely to snatch fourth place from the disappointing Captain Dibble.

Minutes later an excited Pipe told the press, 'Mark did wonders to stay in the saddle after that terrible blunder'. He also admitted, 'I was told off by Riverside Boy's owner Miss Bisgove for telling her the horse had no chance.'

The winning jockey said, 'Fortunately the horse has a long neck, which enabled me to climb back on. I so nearly slid out of the side door.' The late great Fred Rimell had saddled his four winners in the space of thirteen years. Thanks to Bonanza Boy's two wins in 1988 and 1989 and Carvill Hill's victory in 1991 and Run For Free this year, Pipe saddled his four in the space of five years!

One wonders what would have happened had Pipe's top-weighted Chatham, who had been withdrawn after being found lame at the racecourse stables, had been able to run. More than likely, Pipe would have done a Michael Dickinson and had the first five home! But just for good measure Pipe trained four of the other five winners on the Chepstow racecard making it a truly memorable day.

That day I thought Miinnehoma, owned by comedian Freddie Starr, looked so forlorn standing all alone in the unsaddling enclosure after his brave effort and with no one there to greet him. Still, if my memory serves me correctly, Freddie Starr was also absent at Liverpool the day Miinnehoma won the 1994 Aintree National.

Run For Free won one of the most remarkable races ever when later in the season he landed the Scottish Grand National after being left twenty or thirty lengths at the start. He was so far behind and going nowhere that Perrett had seriously considered pulling him up. Despite being hampered when stable mate Riverside Boy fell six from home, Perrett somehow or other managed to win the race by a neck after riding a tremendous finish. Perrett, who had ridden his first winner some twelve years earlier, won a number of other big races besides and

Carvill's Hill, winner of the 1991 race, takes a jump in the 1992 Cheltenham Gold Cup.

these included the Welsh Champion Hurdle, Topham Trophy, Mackeson Gold Cup and the *Daily Express* Triumph Hurdle.

Monday 28 December   £24,248   Three miles, five furlongs and 110 yards

1	Run For Free (M. Pipe)	8-10-9	Mark Perrett
2	Riverside Boy (M. Pipe)	9-10-0	M. Foster
3	Minnehoma (M. Pipe)	9-10-11	J. Lower

Winning owner Mrs Millicent Freethy

11 ran.   Distances: 8l, 5l, 3½l.   SP 11/4 jt. fav., 50/1, 11/4 jt. fav.

Going soft.

Run For Free, bay gelding by Deep Run-Credit Card

1993

Only eight horses faced the starter in 1993 for what could only be described as a sub-standard Welsh Grand National. On this occasion, Martin Pipe had only one representative which was the previous year's runner-up Riverside Boy. Just as Carvill's Hill and Run For Free had done, Riverside Boy, the 6/4 favourite led from start to finish, winning by twenty lengths from Fiddler's Pike, partnered by Rosemary Henderson, with the 1990 winner, Cool Ground, a further eight lengths back. Jenny Pitman's Willsford finished fourth.

Having jumped superbly throughout, Riverside Boy had the race won some way from home. But, for one scary moment, when negotiating the bend nearest the stables, Riverside Boy appeared to show signs of wanting to duck out but the champion jockey Richard Dunwoody was having none of it.

'You can never entirely trust him. That's why I didn't ease up on the run to the line', said Dunwoody who was enjoying his first big race success since becoming stable jockey to Pipe. In order to carry the allotted ten stone, Dunwoody spent a couple of hours in the sauna beforehand and had only a turkey sandwich for his Christmas lunch.

Recognised as one of the best National Hunt jockeys of all time, Ulsterman Dunwoody, who rode his first winner in 1983, won the Aintree National on West Tip in 1986 and again in 1994 on Miinnehoma. He also won the Cheltenham Gold Cup on Charter Party in 1988 and the Champion Hurdle on Kribensis. He was champion jockey three consecutive times from 1992 to 1993 and his 1,679 wins over jumps was a record.

Tuesday 28 December   £2,4928   Three miles, five furlongs and 110 yards

1	Riverside Boy (M. Pipe)	10-10-0	Richard Dunwoody
2	Fiddler's Pike (Mrs R. Henderson)	12-10-0	Mrs R. Henderson
3	Cool Ground (D. Elsworth)	11-10-13	P. Holley

Winning owner Bisgrove Partnership

8 ran.   Distances: 20l, 8l, 5l.   SP 6/4 fav., 20/1, 9/4.   Going heavy.

Riverside Boy, chestnut gelding by Funny Man-Tamorina

1994

The Welsh Grand National fixture of 1994, which was to have taken place on Tuesday 27 December, was abandoned owing to the racecourse being water-logged. But thanks to the efforts of Chepstow's clerk of the course, Rodger Farrant and his staff, as well as the British Horse Racing Board, the Welsh Grand National was switched at very short notice to Newbury Racecourse on the following Saturday.

Two of the eight runners were trained by Martin Pipe. Chatam, the top weight, who was a faller and Lord Relic who was pulled up. Course winner Master Oats, confidently ridden by Norman Williamson, was always travelling well throughout and was still on the bridle when he drew clear four fences out to win impressively by twenty lengths from Earth Summit (it could have been more if Williamson had ridden him out). The 1992 Aintree National winner Party Politics was third with the bottom weight, Gold Cap fourth.

Trained by Kim Bailey at Upper Lambourn, Master Oats, who had begun his racing career rather inauspiciously in a maiden point-to-point as a five-year-old (he was tailed off when pulled up at the ninth!) went on to win the 1995 Cheltenham Gold Cup. He was made a 5/1 favourite for the Aintree National but could only finish seventh behind Royal Athlete. A winner of ten of his twenty-one starts, this game and genuine horse who overcame broken blood vessels and other injuries won around £257,000 in prize money.

Saturday 31 December	£25,106		Three miles and six furlongs
1 Master Oats (K.C. Bailey)	8-11-6	Norman Williamson
2 Earth Summit (N.A. Twiston-Davies)	6-10-12	D. Bridgwater
3 Party Politics (N. Gaslee)	10-11-5	M.A. Fitzgerald

Winning owner Mr Paul Matthews

8 ran.   Distances: 20l, 25l, ½l.   SP 5/2 jt. fav., 4/1, 6/1.

Other jt. fav. Lord Relic (pulled up).   Going heavy.

Master Oats, chestnut gelding by Oats-Miss Poker Face

1997

With the 1995 and 1996 editions being abandoned due to frost, Chepstow's clerk of the course, Rodger Farrant, was praying that the Coral Welsh National hoodoo would be broken and that the event would return to Wales once again. This time the worry was the rain over Christmas which threatened Chepstow's bid to stage the race for the first time in four years. Much to Mr Farrant's relief, fourteen horses – four of them Samouri, Indian Tracker, Evangelica and Cyborgo trained by Martin Pipe – made their way to the start of what was to prove a memorable slog in the mud.

Earth Summit, who as a six-year-old had won the Scottish Grand National, went off at 25/1 and, ridden by Tom Jenks, was never out of the first two. After getting the better of a long tussle with Indian Tracker, Earth Summit went on to win by one-and-three-quarters of a length holding off the late challenge of Don Samouri, who threatened to snatch the prize in the final few yards. Samlee was third and Killeshin fourth. Cyborgo, the favourite, was beaten a long way out and was eventually pulled up.

After giving Earth Summit a kiss in the unsaddling enclosure, his jubilant winning jockey Tom Jenks said, 'He'd been up there in front for a long time and was entitled to feel the strain a bit, but he's very brave. This is a great result for me.' It was also a great result for trainer Nigel Twiston- Davies who had been having a lean time of it. He was at Kempton Park where he saddled Kerawi who landed a gamble in the Christmas Hurdle.Earth Summit was owned by a syndicate of six which included former soccer star Ricky George who said, 'Nigel Twiston-Davies has performed a miracle in bringing him back to top form after he had a very bad suspensory tendon injury and Tom Jenks rode a super race.' Unfortunately though, for Jenks that is, he was sidelined through injury when Earth Summit later that season won the Aintree National under Carl Llewellyn and became the first horse to win the English, Scottish and Welsh Grand Nationals.

Saturday 27 December   £30,846   Three miles, five furlongs and 110 yards

1	Earth Summit (N.A. Twiston-Davies)	9-10-13	Tom Jenks
2	Dom Samouri (M. Pipe)	6-10-0	J.A. McCarthy
3	Samlee (P.J. Hobbs)	8-10-5	D. Bridgwater

Winning owner Summit Syndicate
14 ran.   Distances: 1¾l, 10l, 3½l.   SP 25/1, 12/1, 7/1.
Fav. 3/1 Cyborgo (pulled up).   Going heavy
Earth Summit, bay gelding by Celtic Cone-Win Green Hill

1998

The hero of this year's race was the grey Kendal Cavalier who had been transferred in somewhat controversial circumstances from Rod Millman's yard to Nigel Hawke just ten days earlier. The winner of a four-miler at Cheltenham in soft ground a year previously, Kendal Cavalier, ridden by Barry Fenton, had battled to stay in touch on the first circuit and did not seem to be making much progress. Even so, the testing conditions suited him admirably and as the race went on, the field of sixteen runners was being reduced so much that by the time the third last fence had been reached there were only three horses ahead of him – Eudipe, Fiddling The Facts and Forest Ivory.

Barry Fenton sensing victory sent him ahead and taking the last three obstacles in fine style went some three or four lengths clear on the run-in and was able to withstand the last desperate challenge of Fiddling The Facts to score by half-a-length. Forest Ivory gaining third place and Eudipe fourth and the previous year's winner Earth Summit was pulled up.

Nigel Hawke, who had won the 1991 Aintree National on Seagram and whose riding career had come to an end after a crashing fall at Newton Abbot, had taken out a trainers' licence three years earlier and Kendal Cavalier was his first winner for 241 days. He said, 'We have just messed about with him and he seems to have enjoyed that, but most credit must go to Rod whose place is about twenty-five miles from mine. Kendal Cavalier was going to run at Cheltenham on New Year's day but when the rains came we knew this would be a real test of stamina.'

Kendal Cavalier's owner, Mr Michael Wingfield Digby, when questioned about the change of trainers remarked, 'Moving the horse so close to the race was a gamble, but we felt he would be happier in a smaller yard.'

Monday 28 December   **£34,935**   **Three miles, five furlongs and 110 yards**

1	Kendal Cavalier (N.J. Hawke)	8-10-0	Barry Fenton
2	Fiddling The Facts (N. Henderson)	7-10-6	M.A. Fitzgerald
3	Forest Ivory (D. Nicholson)	7-10-0	A. Maguire

Winning owner Mr Michael Wingfield Digby
14 ran.   Distances: ½l, 5l, 6l.   SP 14/1, 11/2, 14/1.
Fav. 9/2 Earth Summit (pulled up).
Kendal Cavalier, grey gelding by Roselier-Kenda (Bargello)

1999

The first three last year – Kendal Cavalier, Fiddling The Facts and Forest Ivory plus the 1997 winner Earth Summit – all came under starters' orders again this year. On the card it looked as though it was going to be a competitive race. But Henry Daly's seven-year-old Edmund, who had already won twice over the course at Chepstow, completed a hat-trick when making every post a winning one in the capable hands of Richard Johnson.

Forest Ivory some ten lengths down at the winning post, was second ahead of Earthmover with Flaked Oats in fourth. The previous year's winner Kendal Cavalier was fifth and the favourite Young Kenny sixth. Fiddling The Facts was pulled up and Earth Summit, who finished in ninth and last place, was found to have sustained another leg injury and was retired.

Originally trained by Captain Tim Forster, who had trained three Aintree National winners, and who had died earlier in the year, Edmund was now trained by Henry Daly who had taken over his Ludlow yard. In reference to Foster he said, 'He would have enjoyed this. He loved proper chases in hock-deep mud.' A lot of the credit for Edmund's tremendous run must go to his enterprising rider who was sporting a bright yellow haircut. Richard Johnson's hair was dyed that colour as part of a fund raising scheme or dare in aid of stricken fellow jockey Scott Taylor. Those of us who had seen Johnson ride in Welsh point-to-points a few years earlier had no doubts at all that he was destined for the big time.

Tuesday 28 December   **£40,300**   **Three miles, five furlongs and 110 yards**

1 Edmund (H.D. Daly)	7-10-0	Richard Johnson
2 Forest Ivory (A. King)	8-10-0	W. Marston
3 Earthmover (P. Nicholls)	8-10-9	J. Tizzard

Winning owner Lady Knutsford

16 ran.   Distances: 10l, 3½l, 2½l.   Fav. 5/2 Young Kenny (6th).   Going heavy.

Edmund, bay gelding by Video Rock (Fr)-Galia 111 (Fr)

Carl Llewellyn who won the 1998 Aintree Grand National on Earth Summit. Picture by Carl Burrows.

In 2000, Charlie Mann's Moral Support, a winner of his previous four races, was made a 2/1 favourite to win the Coral Eurobet Welsh National. But it was pint size Jocks Cross, ridden by nineteen-year-old conditional jockey Brian Crowley, who bravely battled home to beat the favourite by two-and-a-half lengths.

Edmund, successful twelve months previously, finished an exhausted thirty lengths third with Ambleside in fourth. The third and fourth had made most of the early running with Suny Bay, Moral Support and Jocks Cross not far behind. Even so, going down the back straight for the final time Moral Support took over the lead closely followed by Jocks Cross who then jumped to the front four fences from home. Moral Support tried hard to peg him back but was always fighting a losing battle.

Jocks Cross, who was reversing the form with Moral Support who had beaten him by three-and-a-half lengths in the Rehearsal Chase at Chepstow earlier in the month, returned to the winners' enclosure with blood pouring from his nose. His trainer, Miss Venetia Williams, revealed that he had broken a blood vessel on one other occasion at Punchestown and said, 'Jocks Cross jumped fantastic and Brian gave him a lovely ride.' She added, 'I never dreamt that he could beat the second.'

Crowley said, 'That was great and is without doubt my best win. I could see that Tony Dobbin was getting anxious on Moral Support and I knew my horse would stay every yard. I only had to ask him for one final effort.'

Of the nineteen runners that had set out only nine of them finished the race and three of those non-finishers were trained by Martin Pipe.

Wednesday 27 December   £43,500   Three miles, five furlongs and 110 yards

1	Jocks Cross (Miss V. Williams)	9-10-7	Brian Crowley
2	Moral Support (C. Mann)	8-10-4	A. Dobbin
3	Edmund (H. Daly)	8-10-10	R. Johnson

Winning owner Mrs Gill Harrison

19 ran.   Distances: 2½l, 30l, 17l.   SP 14/1, 2/1 fav., 5/1.

Going heavy, soft in places.

Jocks Cross, chestnut gelding by Riberetto-Shuil Le Dia.

2001

Leighton Aspell's racing career was put on hold when he was arrested as part of farcical, long-running race-fixing investigations – all those involved were eventually exonerated. Aspell had cause to smile again, however, when he won the 2001 Welsh Grand National on the Pat Murphy-trained Supreme Glory. Four fences from home five horses were in with a shout, but soon afterwards it became clear that the race rested between the previous year's winner Jocks Cross and Supreme Glory. However, Aspell had his mount jumping better and they landed over the last in front and went on to withstand the persistent challenge of Jocks Cross to win by two lengths. Bindaree under Carl Llewellyn was a further six lengths away in third place. Martin Pipe's Take Control, who was made favourite, could only manage sixth place.

Pat Murphy had had a traumatic time over the previous year. He suffered the loss of his daughter, Melissa, who died in a road accident, followed by the break-up of his long-time marriage to his wife Louise. As if that wasn't bad enough, his stable star Shooting Light was transferred to Martin Pipe's yard and proceeded to win three races on the trot. Murphy was full of praise for Aspell and said, 'Leighton gave the horse a very positive ride and I just think he's an underated jockey as he rides so many poor horses that can't win, but he never lets you down on the big day.'

Questioned about Shooting Light's departure he replied, 'After he won the Tripleprint Gold Cup at Cheltenham someone phoned me and said it must have been painful to lose a horse like that. I told them that the day before I had sat by my daughter's grave on what should have been her fifteenth birthday. That's what pain is all about, not watching horses run in races!' The Welsh Grand National had been Supreme Glory's target ever since he had finished a good third in a huge field of thirty runners in the Scottish Grand National won by Gingembre last April. But Murphy said, 'I didn't dare back my horse the way my luck had been running.'

Friday 27 December   £43,500   Three miles, five furlongs and 110 yards

1	Supreme Glory (P.G. Murphy)	8-10-0	Leighton Aspell
2	Jocks Cross (Miss V. Williams)	10-10-4	B.J. Crowley
3	Bindaree (N. Twiston-Davies)	7-10-2	C. Llewellyn

Winning owner C.J.L. Moorsom
13 ran.   Distances: 2l, 6l.   SP 10/1, 10/1, 4/1.
Fav. 9/4 Take Control (6th).   Going good to soft, soft in places.
Supreme Glory, bay gelding by Supreme Leader-Pentlows (Sheer Grit)

Race Records

MOST WINS (HORSE)
3 Lacatoi (1935, 1937, 1939)
2 Razorbill (1908, 1911)
2 Miss Balscadden (1926, 1928)
2 Limonali (1959, 1961)
2 Bonanza Boy (1988, 1989)

MOST WINS (OWNER)
5 Mr J.V. Rank (1934, 1935, 1937, 1938, 1939)
2 Mrs G.R. Lewis (1959, 1961)
2 Mr S. Dunster (1988, 1989)

MOST WINS (TRAINER)
5 M. Pipe (1988, 1989, 1991, 1992, 1993)
4 G. Evans (1934, 1935, 1937, 1938)
4 T.F. Rimell (1957, 1968, 1970, 1976)
3 I. Anthony (1930, 1933, 1937)
3 Mrs J. Pitman (1982, 1983, 1986)
2 M. Lindsay (1926, 1928)
2 Earl Jones (1962, 1974)
2 N. Crump (1951, 1980)

TRAINED FIRST FOUR FINISHERS
M. Pipe   1991

TRAINED FIRST AND SECOND
I. Anthony   1936
Mrs J. Pitman   1986 (also trained the 4th)

TRAINED FIRST AND THIRD
I. Anthony   1930
Mrs M. Dickinson   1984
M. Pipe   1991 (also trained the 4th)

MOST WINS (JOCKEY)
4 J. Fawcus (1934, 1935, 1937, 1939)
4 P. Scudamore (1985, 1988, 1989, 1991)

3   D. Nicholson (1959, 1960, 1961)
2   Mr A.W. Wood (1899, 1906)
2   D. Williams (1930, 1933)
2   A. Mullins (1950, 1952)
2   R. Francis (1949, 1956)
2   T. Biddlecombe (1965, 1970)
2   P. Cowley (1963, 1971)
2   K. White (1967, 1974)
2   J. Francome (1980, 1983)
2   G. Bradley (1984, 1986)

SUCCESSFUL AS JOCKEY AND TRAINER
I. Anthony rode Razorbill (1911) and trained Boomlet (1930), Pebble Ridge (1933) and Sorley Boy (1937)

MOST WINS (SIRE)
3   Yutoi (1935, 1937, 1939)
2   Red Prince II (1908, 1911)
2   Balscadden (1926, 1928)
2   Cottage (1936, 1948)
2   Hyder Ali (1959, 1961)
2   Harwell (1968, 1982)
2   Sir Lark (1988, 1989)
2   Roselier (1991, 1998)
Note: Cottage, Harwell and Roselier are the only sires to win the race with two of their progeny.

LARGEST WINNING MARGIN
A distance	Miss Balscadden, 1928
20 lengths	Corbiere, 1982
20 lengths	Carvill's Hill, 1991
20 lengths	Riverside Boy, 1993
20 lengths	Master Oats, 1994

DEAD HEAT
Between Succubus and General Fox, 1914
Note: Succubus won the run-off.

SHORTEST WINNING MARGIN
Short head	Lacatoi beat Waving Star, 1939
Head	Roman Candle beat Timothy Titus, 1909
Head	Razorbill beat Flaxen, 1911
Head	Miss Balscadden beat Postino, 1926
Head	Skyreholme beat Fighting Line, 1951
Head	Crudwell beat Billy Budd, 1956

HIGHEST PRICED WINNERS
25/1   Pattered, 1974
25/1   Earth Summit, 1997
20/1   Miss Balscadden, 1928
20/1   Monaleen, 1955
20/1   Oscar Wilde, 1958
20/1   Deblin's Green, 1973

SHORTEST PRICED WINNERS
1/3   Gangbridge, 1901
10/11   Timber Wolf, 1938
evens   Deerstalker, 1895
6/4   Bloomer, 1900
6/4   Glenrocky, 1905
6/4   Caubeen, 1910
6/4   Pebble Ridge, 1933
6/4   Riverside Boy, 1993

SHORTEST PRICED LOSERS
8/13   Dick Dunn, lost run-off after dead-heating in 1914
4/6   Golden Miller, 3rd in 1936
8/11   Captain John, 4th in 1982

MOST OPEN RENEWAL
11/2 the field in 1974

FAVOURITES
29 favourites (including 5 joint-favourites) successful in 83 renewals (32%)

MOST CONSECUTIVE WINNING FAVOURITES
4   1991-1994 (includes joint-favourites in 1992 and 1994)

MOST CONSECUTIVE LOSING FAVOURITES
6   1972-1980, 1982-1987

FASTEST WINNING TIME
7m.24.0   Creeola II 1957

SLOWEST WINNING TIME
8m.44.8   Riverside Boy   1993
Note: Apart from 1951, I have not been able to identify times for renewals between 1895 and 1954.

LARGEST FIELD
24   1974
23   1981
21   1929

SMALLEST FIELD
3   1938
4   1901, 1906, 1914

HIGHEST WINNING WEIGHTS
12st 10lb   Bloomer, 1900
12st 9lb   Razorbill, 1911
12st 1lb   Vaulx, 1925

LOWEST WINNING WEIGHTS
9st 7lb   Miss Balscadden, 1926
9st 7lb   Miss Balscadden, 1928
9st 7lb   Monaleen, 1955

OLDEST WINNING HORSE
13 years   Snipe's Bridge 1927

YOUNGEST WINNING HORSES
5 years   Nat Gould   1899
              Razorbill   1908
              Jacobus   1912

WINNING AGES
8 years   23 wins
7 years   17 wins
10 years   16 wins
9 years   12 wins
5 years   3 wins
6 years   3 wins
11 years   3 wins
12 years   2 wins
13 years   1 win
aged (7+)   3 wins

WINNING MARES
Miss Balscadden   (1926, 1928)
Miss Gaynus   (1932)
Dinton Lass   (1952)
Clover Bud   (1960)
Rainbow Battle   (1964)

WINNING ENTIRE
Caubeen (1910)

TRAINERS - MOST RUNNERS IN RACE
30   M. Pipe
20   T.F. Rimell
20   Mrs J. Pitman
16   Capt J.B. Powell
16   I. Anthony
14   Hon. A. Hastings
14   J. Roberts
13   J.A.C. Edwards
13   J. Gifford
12   D. Harrison
12   R. Armytage
12   P.J. Hobbs
11   G.B. Balding
10   D. Barons
10   N.A. Twiston-Davies
 9   P. Woodland
 8   F. Hartigan
 8   G.R. Owen
 8   F. Cundell
 8   Capt T. Forster

JOCKEYS - MOST RIDES IN RACE
11   W. Parvin
11   M. Scudamore
10   D. Morgan
 8   D. Nicholson
 8   R. Rowe
 7   R. Burford
 7   S. Mellor
 7   S. Smith Eccles
 7   B. de Haan
 7   B. Powell
 7   R. Dunwoody
 7   R. Francis
 7   P. Scudamore

MOST APPEARANCES IN THE RACE
5   Bonanza Boy (1988-92)
5   Limonali (1959, 1961, 1963-65)
5   Pencoed (1921-23, 1925, 1926)

4   Chavara (1961, 1963-65)
4   Cool Ground (1989-91, 1993)
4   Earth Summit (1994, 1997-99)
4   Klaxton (1949, 1952-54)
4   Peaty Sandy (1981, 1982, 1984, 1985)
4   Silver Grail (1930-33)
4   The Bell (1958-60, 1963)

FATALITIES

Barnecide	1895
Ben Armine	1895
Sandy Shore	1950
Border Lay	1957
Shavings	1963
Mr Jones	1965
Master Brutus	1981
Papa Kharisma	2000

Note: Fatalities as a percentage of all runners = 0.81 per cent.

BIBLIOGRAPHY

The Longsdale Library of Steeplechasing (Many Authorities, Seeley Service & Co.Ltd., London).

Brown Jack (R C Lyle, Putnam, London,1934).

Queen of the Turf: The Dorothy Paget Story (Quinton Gilbey, Arthur Barker Ltd., London, 1973).

The Cheltenham Gold Cup (John Welcome, Pelham Books,London, 1973).

Steeplechase Jockeys: The Great Ones (Tim Fitzgeorge-Parker, Pelham Books, London, 1971).

Gentleman Charles: A history of Foxhunting (George T. Burrows, Vinton & Company, London, 1951).

A Race Apart: The History of the Grand National (Reg Green, Hodder & Stoughton, London, 1988).

Fifty Years of Racing at Chepstow (Pat Lucas, H G Walters Ltd., Tenby, 1976).

Encylopaedia of Steeplechasing (Patricia Smyly, Robert Hale,London, 1979)
.

Biographical Encylopaedia of British Flat Racing (Roger Mortimer, Richard Onslow, Peter Willett. Macdonald and Jane's Publishers Ltd., London, 1978)
.

Famous Gentlemen Riders: At Home and Abroad (Charles Adolph Voight, Hutchinson & Co., London, 1925).

One Hundred Grand Nationals (T H Bird, Country Life Ltd, London, 1937).

The Winter Kings (Ivor Herbert & Patricia Smyly, Pelham Books, London, 1968)
.

Sport From Within (Frank Atherton Brown, Hutchinson, London, 1952).

The Turf's Who's Who in Racing 1939 (J. Fairfax Blakesborough).

The History of Steeplechasing (Michael Seth-Smith, Peter Willett, Roger Mortimer, John Lawrence. Michael Joseph, London, 1966).

The Grand National (Clive Graham & Bill Curling. Barrie & Jenkins Ltd., London, 1972).

The Persian War Story (Sid Barnes & Henry Alper, Pelham Books Ltd, London, 1971).

Grand National (Con O'Leary, Rockliff, London, 1945).

Passports To Life (Harry Llewellyn, Hutchinson/Stanley Paul & Co. Ltd., London 1980).

Master of Hounds (Fred Holley & Others, V A Holley, Merthyr Tydfil, 1987).
When Diamonds Were Trumps (Reginald Herbert, Walter Southwood, London, 1906).

The Sport of Queens (Dick Francis, Michael Joseph Ltd., London, 1957).

Timeform Chasers & Hurdlers (Portway Press) various editions.

The author has also drawn material from the following newspapers:
The Sporting Life, Daily Mail, South Wales Echo, South Wales Daily News, The Western Mail, Cardiff & Merthyr Guardian, Cardiff Times, The Weekly Mail and *The Monmouthshire Merlin*.

ABOUT THE AUTHOR

Dubbed 'Historian of the Welsh Turf' by *The Sporting Life*, Brian Lee has been writing about the Welsh horse racing scene since 1966. As a young lad in the early 1950s, he worked for Cardiff Corporation Parks Department as an assistant to the groundsman at Cardiff's Ely Racecourse which closed in 1939.

However, he never thought then that one day he would be writing about the riders and horses that graced the Ely turf. His association with Chepstow Racecourse goes back even further as his late father and his uncle Philip Donovan took him racing there from an early age.

A prolific writer, he has contributed to numerous publications including the now sadly defunct *The Sporting Life, Racing Post, Horse and Hound* and various other newspapers and magazines. He is the author of thirteen books and his first racing book, *The Races Came Off: The story of point-to-point racing in South and West Wales*, was described by *The Sporting Life* as 'utterly delightful and of its kind unique.'

He has been married to his wife Jacqueline for forty-three years and she has no interest at all in horse racing!

Brian Lee with Brian Fletcher who rode three Aintree Grand National winners and who will always be associated with the immortal Red Rum.